Called To Cooperate

A Biblical Survey and Application of Teamwork

Jeff Mingee

I c h t h u s *Publications* · Apollo, Pennsylvania

Our goal is to provide high-quality, thought-provoking books that foster encouragement and spiritual growth. For more information regarding Ichthus Publications, other IP books, or bulk purchases, visit us online or write to adam@ichthuspublications.com.

Printed in the United States of America.

Called to Cooperate: A Biblical Survey and Application of Teamwork
Library of Congress Control Number: 2016934541
ISBN 13: 978-0-9973589-0-2

www.ichthuspublications.com

Praise for *Called To Cooperate*

"Jeff is both a theologian and a practitioner on this subject. He's smart and practical as he presents the goodness of gospel partnership. As a successful church planter himself, he's the right guy to remind the church that 'teamwork' and 'partnership' were not invented in the boardroom."

—**Clint Clifton**, North American Mission Board, Send D.C. Coordinator

"Far too many leaders tackle their tasks as lone rangers, assuming they can reach their goals on their own. That approach to leadership is draining, if not dangerous. In this book, Jeff Mingee unpacks a better approach—teamwork—from a biblical perspective. Because the spiritual battles leaders face are real and intense, it is imperative that we learn the truths in this work."

—**Dr. Chuck Lawless**, Dean of Graduate Studies at Southeastern Baptist Theological Seminary and author of *Nobodies for Jesus: 14 Days Towards a Great Commission Lifestyle*

"Working together to advance the gospel is more than theory to Jeff Mingee. As a church planter, Jeff has firsthand experience of helping people to embrace their calling to cooperate for the cause of Christ. Jeff is both a learner and a leader, with a passion to see disciples made that become disciple makers."

—**Dr. Brian Autry**, Executive Director, Southern Baptist Conservatives of Virginia

"The church should be leading the way in developing and utilizing teams. Far too often the church celebrates the unity of the Trinity while fighting for individualistic ministry needs. Jeff hasn't written a theoretical book on teams. He's written a teamwork manifesto that all church leaders should take advantage of."

—**Rob Shepherd**, Pastor of Next Level Church and author of *Even If You Were Perfect Someone Would Crucify You*

"Robust Biblical theology is the foundation for all that the church is and does. In *Called To Cooperate*, Jeff aptly demonstrates the implications of the gospel for partnership and teamwork among God's people. The unity of the bride of Christ will be enhanced as leaders implement the principles found in this book."

—**Matt Rogers**, Pastor of The Church at Cherrydale and author of *Aspire* and *Seven Arrows for Bible Reading*

"This was uplifting, clarifying, and thought-provoking. I found myself stopping and praying about things I would like to see God do in me and my team here. I love the emphasis on the biblical worldview or theology of teamwork. Jeff offers substantial scriptural support that is effective in supporting his premise. The book would be a valuable tool in the hands of others in Christian education. Teachers could incorporate the truths in their roles as mentors to junior high and high school students."

—**Lori Rogers**, Principal, Calvary Classical School, Hampton, Virginia

"Jeff is spot on with his reminder of the dangers of isolation, especially as it relates to making disciples and planting churches. He rightly argues that the gospel not only unites as family, but calls us to work together for something much greater than ourselves. I highly recommend this book to anyone pastoring or planting a church."

—**Micah Millican**, North American Mission Board, Director of Church Planter Relations

"In *Called To Cooperate*, Jeff outlines the important biblical necessity for Christian teamwork. Whether in the marketplace, church leadership, or other pursuits, we all serve a God who has expressed himself to us as a cooperating God. Jeff shows us how our own internal pursuits of teamwork and cooperation are a holy task. This is a great work for anyone who seeks to lead using this biblical model."

—**Rev. Chad Brooks**, Pastor of Foundry and Host of "The Productive Pastor" Podcast

For Lauren, Aiden, and Carter, and the incredible people with whom I've had the honor of serving on teams. I'm a better follower of Jesus because of you.

Contents

Foreword

VERY EARLY ON in the Bible, we learn that being alone is not a good thing (Gen. 1:18). Moses tried to handle the entire burden of leading the Israelites on his own; it took a rebuke from his father-in-law Jethro before he saw that what he was doing was unsustainable (Exod. 18:13-23). He needed a team. David had his mighty men. The apostle Paul traveled with trusted ministry companions. Even the Lord Jesus did not attempt to engage in ministry on his own, but he surrounded himself with a group of disciples who could assist him and carry on the work after his departure.

But sadly, the landscape of the evangelical church in America is littered with examples of territorial pastors isolating themselves from other gospel workers. You have probably heard horror stories of leaders who treated their staff like servants, chewing them up and spitting them out when they were no longer useful. It is not for nothing that we have a stereotype of the competitive pastor who views the successes of other congregations as a threat to his church. Many church leaders lack a vision for sacrificially laboring to see other leaders raised up and sent out into the harvest fields. Many churches fail to grasp the fact that when one church receives a blessing, the entire Church of God should rejoice. As a result, ministries crack under their own weight, leaders burn out quickly, and fruitful work does not survive from one generation to the next.

Why is this so? If the heroes of our faith saw the benefit of teamwork, why do so many pastors today isolate themselves from others? In this book, Jeff Mingee offers several possible diagnoses: pride, fear, and indifference. But he also offers a compelling vision of what it can look like to live and work in joyful teams, sharing the difficulties and successes of ministry with others that we love.

I have to admit that before I read this book, I had not really given much thought to the biblical basis for working in teams. But Jeff walks the reader through the Bible, making a case for cooperation and partnership from the nature of the ontological Trinity, the message of the gospel, and the principles of Wisdom. Going forward, I do not think I will be able to read my Bible without seeing teamwork on almost every page.

If you are holding this book in your hand (or looking at it on your e-reader), then it is safe to assume that you are either a team leader, a team member, or you need to become one. In whatever situation you find yourself, you can be sure that this short resource will be a blessing to you. Get started now and begin to reap the blessings of teamwork in your context.

Mike McKinley
Sterling, VA

ONE

The Gospel and Teamwork

"Whether or not one realizes it, the gospel is, by its very nature, intensely social."

—Mark Liederbach[1]

You matter to God. And, as we say in the South, "Y'all matter to God." In calling you to himself, God has called you to cooperation and teamwork with others. He's called you to community and partnership. From community and accountability groups to ministry volunteer teams and Sunday school classes, every step in our walk of faith leads us into the context of teams. We enjoy the fellowship of other believers during worship. We embrace—or are occasionally coerced into—our common responsibility, and we agree to serve on the school board, the homeowners association, or the leadership team. We learn from the beginning that "there is no such thing as the lone-ranger Christian," and are taught to embrace the paradigm that "where two or three are gathered" a good thing

---

[1] Liederbach and Reid, *Convergent Church*, 214.

must be happening. We nod with understanding that "a chord of three strands is not easily broken." These truths make practical and pragmatic sense to us. We are better together than we are on our own. But to our impairment we have failed to develop a theology of teamwork. We work on staff teams, we volunteer on ministry teams and committees, we play on teams, we gather in teams; but we don't know what God says about teams. Teams matter to God.

A familiarity with Scripture exposes our folly. In the beginning, God the Father works with God the Son and God the Holy Spirit, as a team, in creation. In Genesis 2 we see the theological foundations of teamwork as God himself declared, "it is not good that the man should be alone" (Gen. 2:18). In Exodus we read of Moses who is sharpened by the advice of Jethro (Exod. 18) and we read of the participation of God's people from Oholiab and Bezalel (Exod. 31) to the cooperative work of the people of Israel in building the Tabernacle (Exod. 36—39). In Numbers we are systematically reminded that the story of salvation is a communal story as we read the census of God's people (Num. 1, 26). Recounting Israel's history, David and his mighty men are exemplified (2 Sam. 23), and we hear David's parting wisdom to Solomon to "deal loyally" with those who have helped in times past (1 Kgs. 2:1-9). We see the poignant example of Jonah who thought that a relationship with God excused him from community with such people as the Ninevites, rather than understanding that a relationship with God compelled him to such. We ought to work with one another, as Paul did, in this "partnership in the gospel" (Phil. 1:5). We are not meant to work alone. The triune God, from creation to redemption, has operated in teamwork and calls us to teamwork. God, in calling you to himself, likewise calls you to teamwork.

Teamwork is from God. The Bible tells me so. While ministry teams that read and discuss the latest secular business books may gain great counsel on how to work better as a team, they will never learn the theological foundation of teamwork apart from Scripture. Those of us who are Christians and who work or serve—or desire to work or serve—in the context of teams must see teamwork as primarily theological and biblical. We must search the Scripture for the why's and how's of teamwork. To dismiss the written Word is to dismiss the Author, God. To dismiss the written Word is to dismiss the Subject, Jesus. To dismiss the written Word is to dismiss the Holy Spirit, who sanctifies us by the Word. Any understanding of teamwork without the biblical text will be incomplete. As we will see throughout Scripture, God, who calls us to Himself, calls us to teamwork. So what exactly is teamwork?

Teamwork Defined

D. A. Carson, an evangelical theologian and professor of the New Testament, defines Christian fellowship as "self-

19

sacrificing conformity to the gospel."[1] Building on that definition, Christian teamwork could be defined as "self - sacrificing conformity to the gospel for the advancement of the gospel." No matter what field of service your team is in— athletics or education or church or humanitarian or managerial or retail or business—Christian teamwork will require self-sacrificing conformity to the gospel for the advancement of the gospel. Teamwork is cooperating for a common goal. For example, an athletic team works together to get points on the scoreboard. A publishing team comes together to publish a finished manuscript. A team of educators comes together for the purpose of educating. Christian teamwork comes together for the gospel. But the gospel is not merely the goal of Christian teamwork, it is the grounds of Christian teamwork.

The Gospel

"For our sake he (God) made him (Jesus) to be sin who knew no sin, so that in him we might become the righteousness of God" (2 Cor 5:21). This is the gospel. The apostle Paul lamented that his Jewish kinsman did not understand it and sought to achieve righteousness on their own (Rom. 10:1-4). The apostle John wrote that we might believe it and believing have life (John 20:30-31). The apostle Peter realized that this gospel overpowered social divisions (Acts 10). In other words,

---

[1] Carson, *Basics for Believers: An Exposition of Philippians*, 16.

this gospel recreates us and reconciles us through the blood of Christ.

Our righteousness is in Christ, not in ourselves. Our righteousness, or right-ness before a holy God, is not wrapped up in what we do but rather is found in what Christ has done. This is fundamental to living rightly before God. Paul wrote, "the righteous shall live by faith" (Rom. 1:17). We are not the heroes of our righteousness, actively achieving it on our own. We are, instead, humble recipients who, in Christ, become the righteousness of God.

The gospel is the good news of this gifted righteousness. It begins with God creating a good world and giving people good rules by which to enjoy life. But as the sad chapter of Genesis 3 tells us, we traded those good rules for our own way. And we traded the protection of the King for separation from the King. But while we were yet sinners and separated from God he sent Christ to live the life we failed to live and die the death we deserved to die. In our place he stood condemned. And by the triumphant resurrection from the grave God displayed his approval on Jesus. The resurrection etched into a rolled away stone that which God had said, "This is my beloved Son with whom I am well pleased." And this Jesus will be known and worshipped by people from every tribe and nation. He will dwell with his people. He will wipe away every tear and trample every enemy under his feet. The gospel is the good news of the great King.

We cannot appreciate the good news of the gospel without facing the reality of our bad condition. The effects of sin on teams are not hard to discover. Patrick Lencioni points out, "The fact remains that teams, because they are made up of imperfect human beings, are inherently dysfunctional."[1] Have you ever served on a dysfunctional team or on a team with a dysfunctional person? (If you're answer is no, then perhaps you've been the dysfunctional person)! This is not merely the result of our imperfections, but of sin. The anger you feel when your co-worker disagrees with you is a result of sin. The way board members attack each other and gossip about each other are a result of sin. We see in the first effects of sin a blaming between our first parents in the Garden of Eden, Adam and Eve. Have you ever served on a team with people who fought for credit but always shifted blame? It's never their fault; someone else is always to blame. Those moments are clear echoes of Genesis 3.

In Lencioni's *Five Dysfunctions of a Team*, key actions and attitudes are revealed that cause teams to break down. Each of these dysfunctions is a reverberation of Genesis three and the results of sin:

- *Absence of trust seen in refusing to be vulnerable*. After Adam and Eve sinned they tried to cover themselves with fig leaves. They were unwillingly to be truly known

---

[1] Lencioni, *The Five Dysfunctions of a Team*, vii.

because they no longer trusted each other or God. In the same way, teams today are filled with individuals who struggle to trust.

- *Fear of conflict seen in artificial harmony.* Fear entered the world in Genesis 3. Instead of disagreeing graciously and compassionately, after the first sin Adam and Eve feared the graceless conflict that would ensue. Similarly, teams today are often characterized by artificial harmony instead of the willingness to disagree graciously.

- *Lack of commitment seen in ambiguity.* Ambiguity is the language of unfulfilled promises. "It'll get done." "Mistakes were made." Ever since Genesis 3 we've been pulled in multiple directions and our commitment has been blurred by ambiguity.

- *Avoidance of accountability seen in low standards.* God found Adam and Eve hiding in the bushes after the first sin. Unfortunately we've been hiding ever since. Even when we're working together in teams, we hide in our avoidance of accountability.

- *Inattention to results seen in concern for status and ego.* The serpent appealed to Eve's ego. He's covered a lot of ground since then appealing to ours as well. Rather than attention to the results of the team, we're often more concerned with our individual stats and reputation.

We see the effects of sin and the power of the gospel everywhere. This gospel changes us and changes how we interact with others. Having a righteousness that is independent of our performance, we are only then able to become interdependent with others; especially those who also have found their righteousness in Christ. We are reconciled to God and to those whom God has reconciled to himself.

God's design in salvation is to reconcile a people to himself; and in so doing, he reconciles those people to one another. Paul wrote of this reconciling gospel to the Ephesians,

> "Therefore remember that at one time you Gentiles in the flesh, called 'the uncircumcision' by what is called the circumcision, which is made in the flesh by hands—12 remember that you were at that time separated from Christ, alienated from the commonwealth of Israel and strangers to the covenants of promise, having no hope and without God in the world. 13 But now in Christ Jesus you who once were far off have been brought near by the blood of Christ. 14 For he himself is our peace, who has made us both one and has broken down in his flesh the dividing wall of hostility 15 by abolishing the law of commandments expressed in ordinances, that he might create in himself one new man in place of the two, so making peace, 16 and might reconcile us both to God in one body through the cross, thereby killing the hostility. 17 And he came and preached peace to you

who were far off and peace to those who were near.
[18] For through him we both have access in one Spirit to
the Father. [19] So then you are no longer strangers and
aliens, but you are fellow citizens with the saints and
members of the household of God, [20] built on the
foundation of the apostles and prophets, Christ Jesus
himself being the cornerstone, [21] in whom the whole
structure, being joined together, grows into a holy
temple in the Lord. [22] In him you also are being built
together into a dwelling place for God by the Spirit"
(Eph. 2:11-22).

The gospel leads us to community. The dividing wall of
hostility has been broken down. The Lord Jesus is creating one
new man. We are now fellow citizens being built together into a
holy temple. The gospel leads us to teamwork. When we fail to
appreciate this, we fail to appreciate the richness of the gospel.
To treat salvation as though it reconciles us to God but not to
other believers is to cheapen salvation. We do not have a one-
dimensional gospel but a gospel that reconciles every
dimension.

And yet, church staff teams and pastoral leadership teams
struggle for lack of a theology of teamwork. Church planting
launch teams are being built into "gospel-centered
communities" while an inability to articulate how the gospel
drives their teamwork prevents full growth. (And try planting a
church without teamwork)! We converse about teamwork from
a pragmatic and practical standpoint. And while ministry and

teamwork are certainly practical and pragmatic, they are inherently theological.

We can no longer afford to operate in teams without developing a theology of teamwork. If our teams are going to be driven by, and leave behind, a deep appreciation for the banner "*Soli Deo Gloria*, To God alone be the glory," we must work to see God's glory in our teams. We must labor to understand how the gospel impacts our teams. We must get to the theological foundations—the God-centeredness—of teamwork.

As we develop a theology of teamwork, we will find ourselves worshipping more fully the God who created us and called us. We will find ourselves enjoying his glory as we work with others for the good of the church and the cities in which we live. As we develop a theology of teamwork we will come to better understand what it means to be together for the gospel.

Ethics professor Mark Liederbach explains,

> "Whether or not one realizes it, the gospel is—by its very nature—intensely social. It is given to people for the benefit of people and is expected to have an impact not only on individuals but also on the world in which they live."[1]

---

[1] Liederbach and Reid, 214.

The Gospel Frees Us to Teamwork

This good news frees us to teamwork. Imagine for a moment being on a team with someone who had not experienced the gospel. Now imagine the ways they would inevitably manipulate others for their own personal gain. You could certainly envision the ways they would discredit others in order to look more credible themselves. Many of us don't have to imagine these things; we've been through them at least once. And, unfortunate as it is to say, many of us have been such a team member ourselves. The tragic reality is that all of us were born this way. Such brokenness is inherent in our constitution and makeup. It defines who we are from the very beginning.

But here's the good news: the gospel frees us to teamwork.

- Because we have God's full approval in the gospel we no longer have to manipulate the people around us or our teams, seeking the approval of others.
- Because we have the riches of grace in Christ Jesus, we no longer have to cheat others as we strain for an advantage.
- Because we have been reconciled to God through the work of Christ, we no longer need to seek prestige in the opinion of others on the merits of our own work.

God, in his gift of common grace, can and does give us good team members who are not always fellow Christians. He sometimes surrounds us with people who, though they are not professing Christians, are nonetheless honest and law abiding in their business ethics and generous in their personal dealings. Yet, without Christ, all of us are following the "spirit that is now at work in the sons of disobedience" (Eph. 2:2). Without the saving grace of God we are by nature self-serving and enemies of God. But in Christ we who were once far off have been drawn near. In the gospel we have been made new. And this gospel frees us to teamwork.

The Gospel Compels Us to Teamwork

The gospel, however, does not merely open up the possibility of teamwork. The gospel actively compels us to teamwork. We say with Paul,

> "For the love of Christ controls us, because we have concluded this: that one has died for all, therefore all have died; and he died for all, that those who live might no longer live for themselves but for him who for their sake died and was raised" (2 Cor. 5:14-15).

Yes, we live for him who died for us. Such a display of love grips us and governs us. It becomes not only our model, but also our motivation. We are controlled, or compelled, by the love of Christ. We, having been reconciled with God, have been given "the ministry of reconciliation" and have become "ambassadors for Christ" (2 Cor. 5:18-20). And this ministry is a call to teamwork. Pastor and church planter Tim Chester noted,

> "Into our pervasively individualistic worldview, we speak the gospel message of reconciliation, unity, and identity as the people of God. This is perhaps the most significant 'culture gap' that the church has to bridge. . . . My being in Christ means being in Christ with those who are in Christ."[1]

The liberating love of Christ does not simply open us up to the possibility of teamwork, it actively compels us to teamwork. If we claim to be gripped by the gospel, we must be active participants in gospel teamwork. We hear this in Paul's opening words to the believers in Philippi:

> "I thank my God in all my remembrance of you, always in every prayer of mine for you all making my prayer with joy, because of your partnership in the gospel from the first day until now. . . . It is right for me to feel this way about you all, because I hold you in my heart, for you are all partakers with me of grace" (Phil 1:3-4, 7).

The apostle Paul wrote, with chained hands and a free heart, of his love for his fellow believers. Undoubtedly Paul thought of the Philippian Jailer whom he had baptized, the slave girl whom

---

[1] Timmis, *Total Church*, 41.

he had seen delivered, and Lydia who faithfully served as a minister of the gospel (Acts 16). At the end of Paul's letter to the Philippians he would call Euodia and Syntyche to "agree in the Lord" (Phil. 4:2). Paul knew that this gospel was creating a new society, a new team—and he thanked God for it. Paul, in light of the gospel, called them to teamwork.

British theologian and author John Stott observed,

> "God intends his people to be a visual model of the gospel, to demonstrate before people's eyes the good news of reconciliation. But what is the good of gospel campaigns if they do not produce gospel churches?"[1]

The apostle Paul labors in Ephesians 3 to help us see how the grace of God leads us to be active participants in the community of faith known as the church. Grace, Paul explains, was given to him so that he could preach Christ to the Gentiles so that "through the church the manifold wisdom of God might now be made known to the rulers and authorities in the heavenly places" (Eph. 3:10). The gospel of grace created the church and now grace compels us to active participation in the church as we display the beauty of the gospel. Grace compels us to teamwork.

As we read the journeys and letters of the apostle Paul we meet a man absolutely defined by the gospel. Every word in Scripture borne by the Spirit and penned by Paul drives us to a greater appreciation for the substitutionary work of Christ. And

---

[1] Stott, *Ephesians*, 111.

every missionary endeavor in which this gospel-saturated man was part points us to teamwork. Not a pragmatic, results-driven, efficiency based teamwork; but rather a theologically informed teamwork, a "partnership in the gospel" (Phil. 1:5).

Those of us who long to be Great Commission Christians must develop a theology of teamwork. If we want to see churches planted and new gospel communities formed, part of our journey will be learning how to work together in a healthy and gospel-centered way. If those of us in leadership want to "equip the saints for the work of the ministry" (Eph. 4:12), then we will do so in the context of intentionally-developed and theologically-informed teams. Let us marvel—as Paul did— that the gospel has saved us. Let us labor to see this gospel advanced. And let us do so, not as lone-ranger Christians, but as those who have developed a healthy and gospel-centered theology of teamwork.

Team Discussion Questions

1. How did this chapter challenge or affirm your thinking about teamwork?

2. Jeff wrote, "the gospel is not merely the goal of Christian teamwork, it is the grounds of Christian teamwork." What practical difference does the gospel make in how you navigate teamwork?

3. Describing how the gospel frees us to teamwork, Jeff listed three specific ways (God's full approval, the riches of grace, and reconciliation). Would you add anything to that list? If not, does one of the listed ways resonate most with you?

4. What is one way that you can begin to approach or treat teamwork differently because of what you learned in this chapter?

TWO

Bearing the Image of a Triune God

"The divine image in man is the reflection of the divine 'us'—that is, the three persons of the Godhead, one in substance and equal in power and glory, living together in unity and eternal love."

—Joel Beeke[1]

The Origin of Teamwork

In the beginning, God created" (Gen 1:1). The original effort and example of teamwork in our world—creation— was perhaps the most beautiful that ever has been or ever will be. Products of great human teamwork, such as the pyramids of ancient Egypt or the construction of the Brooklyn Bridge, pale in comparison. The accomplishments of elite athletic teams such as the "Miracle on Ice" 1980 United States Olympic hockey team, are nothing next to the cooperation in creation. God the Father, God the Son, and God the Holy Spirit created all that is, together. God the Father did not speak or create

---

[1] Beeke, *Friends and Lovers: Cultivating Companionship and Intimacy in Marriage*, Kindle location 207.

without the Son and the Spirit. The Son and the Spirit did not create independent of the Father. Creation was a team effort.

But creation was by no means the first team-oriented action of God. That would be love. And love existed long before creation. Jesus speaks of the love with which the Father loved him "before the foundation of the world" (John 17:24). British scholar Michael Reeves writes,

> "Here is a God who is not essentially lonely, but who has been loving for all eternity as the Father has loved the Son in the Spirit. Loving others is not a strange or novel thing for this God at all; it is at the root of who he is."[1]

Love was the first team activity—celebrated from eternity past between God the Father, God the Son, and God the Holy Spirit.

Teamwork originates in God. He is the origin of community, creation, and team. He is the One who displays fellowship, team, and love; and the One to whom those of us who would rightly understand such things must look. But don't we seemingly tend to look everywhere else? When we think about teamwork we look at the individuals on the team, we consider attitudes that impact the team, we work to create common goals that the team can pursue together, we gain an understanding through personality profiles that reveal habits

---

[1] Reeves, *Delighting in the Trinity*, 41.

and traits. We tend to look all around and even within, but fail to look up.

When we begin a conversation about teamwork anywhere other than with God as the starting point, we build on a faulty foundation. Instead, we must begin with the triune nature of God.

If God were not triune in nature, we would perhaps never have a conversation about teamwork. Or if we did consider the topic, we would do so based on a utilitarian foundation (the ends justify the means), rather than a Trinitarian foundation. But for the Christian, the Trinity is a critical part of this conversation. The Trinity has serious and wonderful implications. Again, to quote Michael Reeves,

> ". . . the triune nature of this God affects everything from how we listen to music to how we pray: it makes for happier marriages, warmer dealings with others, better church life; it gives Christians assurance, shapes holiness and transforms the very way we look at the world around us."[1]

God's triune nature shapes everything including how we treat the complicated topic of teamwork. Noted theologian Bruce Ware writes,

---

[1] *Ibid.*,10.

"The eternal relationality of the Father, Son, and Spirit calls for, and calls forth, a created community of persons—not isolated individuals who exist in close proximity, but interconnected and interdependent relational persons in community."[1]

Does that sound like your experience? Are the teams you currently serve on, or have served on in the past, "interconnected and interdependent relational persons in community?" Hardly. Even as a leader on a team, I've often felt isolated and alone. I've looked around and thought, *everyone on this team is on a completely different page*. Just recently I had a team member—who is one of our lead volunteers—contact me and admit, "Jeff, I feel completely out of the loop on what's happening." I wish I could say she was the first volunteer to tell me that. Now the problem is partly pragmatic and can be solved by more consistent conversations and, in this instance, regular email communication. But I would be amiss if I ignored the reality that we're failing to be the team God would have us to be.

Yes, the Trinity is where we begin our biblical survey about teamwork. There we begin to think about how we positively contribute to our marriage and ministry teams. There we begin our conversations about community conflict, team meetings, and how to be part of a team.

---

[1] "The Trinity." Last Modified January 15, 2008. Accessed February 12, 2015. http://radicalcall.wordpress.com/2008/01/15/the-trinity-bruce-ware/.

Image-Bearing in Teamwork

But how does God being relational affect us? Can't we just say, "Good for him," and go about our own business? Well, no. We can't. We are image bearers, which means we are both called to teamwork *and* called to image forth God in our teamwork. "The God who loves to have an outgoing Image of himself in his Son loves to have many images of his love (who are themselves outgoing)."[1] When God gave dominion to Adam and Eve in the Garden of Eden he didn't just call them to teamwork (though he certainly did that!); he was sending forth image bearers.

As you sit in that staff meeting, as you interact with the secretary down the hall, as you celebrate the victories of those on your team—you are imaging God. With each interaction we are meant to echo the love of this triune God. In fact,

> "Made in the image of this God, we are created to delight in harmonious relationship, to love God, to love each other. Thus Jesus taught that the first and greatest commandment in the law is to love the Lord your God with all your heart and with all your soul and with all your mind, and the second is to love your neighbor as yourself (Mt 22:36-39). That is what we are created for."[2]

---

[1] Reeves, 43.

[2] *Ibid.*, 65.

God's triune nature leads us to love our neighbors, our enemies, ourselves, our co-workers, and more. God's triune nature leads us to be good team members.

What would it look like if God were a member of your team? How would he offer feedback? How would he promote ideas? How would he respond to sin? Now, you're not God (in case you forgot); but you are an image-bearer of this God. You are a display of his love. You ought to paint a clear picture of how God would go about teamwork. You bear his image.

Think about a recent experience you had as part of a team. Perhaps it was a board meeting making major decisions or a teaching team planning out a curriculum map. How did you image God in your teamwork? Were you patient with others? Did you offer encouraging comments and build others up? How did you fail to image God in your teamwork? Did you cross your arms and lean back in your chair refusing to honestly share your thoughts? Did you pull out your phone and focus on something that you cared more about? We are meant to be image bearers.

The Ultimate Aim of Teamwork

Whatever you do, whether you eat or drink (or work on a team), do all to the glory of God (1 Cor. 10:31). The ultimate aim of teamwork is the glory of God. This is true of our teams in the twenty-first century, and it was true of the very first team as the triune God loved in eternity past.

John Piper highlights Jonathan Edwards' explanation that the Trinity is God's displaying himself in the image of his Son and his enjoying himself in the Spirit. Edwards writes, "God is glorified not only by His glory's being seen, but by its being rejoiced in."[1] The ultimate aim of the Trinity is the glory of God. The ultimate aim of our teamwork must be the same.

When we work alongside other people, let us aim for God's glory as we:

- Encourage others when they are struggling.
- Communicate with others about ideas.
- Are frustrated by sin in others and ourselves.
- Celebrate victories.
- Offer and receive criticism.
- Suffer the unrighteous wrath of people.

Most teams don't aim for the glory of God. Most teams—even ministry teams—have a tendency to treat God's glory as an unspoken or assumed goal. God's glory is not meant to be an accidental by-product but the ultimate aim of our teams. The Trinity teaches us that all of our teamwork ought to intentionally aim toward the glory of God.

---

[1] Piper, *A God Entranced Vision of All Things*, 26.

Team Discussion Questions

1. What was one key principle about teamwork that you learned or were reminded of in this chapter?

2. Jeff asked the following questions: "What would it look like if God were a member of your team? How would he offer feedback? How would he promote ideas?" How did this concept resonate with you? How would you answer the questions about God being a member of your team?

3. How do you tend to image God well (or poorly) in your teamwork?

THREE

Moses And . . .
Teamwork in the Life of Moses

"Moses' father-in-law said to him, 'What you are doing is not good. You and the people will certainly wear yourselves out, for the thing is too heavy for you. You are not able to do it alone'" (Exodus 18:17-18).

Leadership matters. Leaders steer the ship and govern the conversation. Their decisions, whether intentional or not, ripple through the organizational chart. Leaders lead. Great leaders know, however, that the people with whom they surround themselves are equally as important as the leader themselves. It's not just "The Leader." Rather, it's "The Leader *and . . .*" Not only does *leadership* matter, *teamwork* matters.

The life of Moses demonstrates the gravity of teamwork. From God's calling of Moses to Moses' passing the baton to Joshua, we hear the repeating refrain, "Moses and . . ."

- Moses *and* Aaron (Exod. 4)
- Moses *and* Eleazar (Num. 31:31)

- Moses *and* the people (Exod. 15:1)
- Moses *and* Jethro (Exod. 18; Deut. 1)
- Moses *and* the elders of Israel (Deut. 27:1)
- Moses *and* Joshua (Deut. 3:28; 31; 34)

Great leaders have great teams. They are not content to operate independent of others; they do not function alone. If you are in leadership, are you aware of the people God has surrounded you with and how they can and have helped you succeed? When was the last time you offered them thanks or publicly recognized their contributions? Conversely, if you are not currently in a position of leadership, are you aware of the difference that you make for the leader? When was the last time you asked how you could relieve a burden or better share some of the workload? When was the last time you went that extra mile for something that mattered greatly *to them*? It's not just *you*, it's "you and . . ."

Moses and Aaron

"But Moses said to the LORD, 'Oh, my Lord, I am not eloquent, either in the past or since you have spoken to your servant, but I am slow of speech and of tongue.' [11] Then the LORD said to him, 'Who has made man's mouth? Who makes him mute, or deaf, or seeing, or blind? Is it not I, the LORD? [12] Now therefore go, and I will be with your mouth and teach you what you shall speak.' [13] But he said, 'Oh, my Lord, please send someone else.' [14] Then the anger of the LORD was

42

kindled against Moses and he said, 'Is there not Aaron, your brother, the Levite? I know that he can speak well. Behold, he is coming out to meet you, and when he sees you, he will be glad in his heart. [15] You shall speak to him and put the words in his mouth, and I will be with your mouth and with his mouth and will teach you both what to do. [16] He shall speak for you to the people, and he shall be your mouth, and you shall be as God to him. [17] And take in your hand this staff, with which you shall do the signs'" (Exod. 4:10-17).

Ask any honest leader and they will tell you that their current leadership role reveals many of their inabilities. Ask any humble leader and they will tell you about the great team with whom they get to work. Professors of Leadership and world-renowned authors James Kouzes and Barry Posner explain,

> "After reviewing thousands of personal-best cases, we developed a simple test to detect whether someone is on the road to becoming a leader. That test is the frequency of the use of the word *we*."[1]

Teamwork is the greenhouse for great leaders.

Moses—either out of fear or self-awareness (and most likely a combination of the two)—wavered before the idea of serving God alone. God gave him Aaron as a co-laborer, but not before Moses begged. It's almost as though God wanted Moses

---

[1] Kouzes and Posner, *The Leadership Challenge* 4th ed., 20.

to feel the depth of his need for teamwork. Moses couldn't go at leading God's people alone; and he wouldn't.

Moses and Aaron display for us the power of plurality in leadership. Where Moses was weak, Aaron was strong. Where Aaron was confused, Moses was clear. God used their cooperation for the purpose of his glory. A great example of this is found in Exodus 17 when God's people went to war with the Amalekites. God had told Moses, "As long as your hands are lifted up, you will achieve victory on behalf of my people. But, if your hands begin to drop, Israel will be overtaken." And so it was. Moses held his hands up and Israel advanced. As he grew tired his arms began to lower. But in his weakness, Moses learned the power of partnership. Aaron and Hur stepped in and upheld Moses' arms. And, in so doing, with Moses' arms outstretched, victory was achieved on behalf of God's people (vs. 8-13).

Moses points us to Jesus, who, with his arms outstretched, achieved victory on behalf of God's people. But Moses wasn't Jesus. And neither are you. Where Jesus alone had to achieve victory over our sin, you cannot achieve victory alone. You need the people God has placed around you. You are as dependent on them as Moses was on Aaron.

There are seasons of life when we are like Moses and need Aaron and Hur around us. There are seasons when we need to surround Moses. When you volunteer on the school board, for instance, you're not just "doing your part," you're coming alongside the teachers and faculty to lift up their arms. As the husband of a four-year-old kindergarten teacher, I know how much my wife appreciates having dedicated and caring people serve on the school board. When the parents in her class step up and say, "I'll be the class parent," or "I'll organize the event," they're not only taking some of the pressure off, they're lifting up her arms. For the past two years I've coached my now seven-year-old son's Upward basketball team, which includes ten first and second graders. I can tell you it feels more like 10,000. It is certainly an incredible help to have parents say, "I'll organize snacks this year." What's more, I've freely admitted that if my good friend Greg wouldn't coach with me, I'm not sure I'd do it! We all need people around us who can lift up our arms, and, conversely, we need to be willing to lift up the arms of those around us.

This isn't just a volunteer issue either. If you're on a staff team, you've been hired to help. It does not—or should not—matter where the person needing assistance falls on the organizational chart in relation to you. You have been hired to help the organization at large, and that means helping the people. Perhaps you have heard of the preacher's illustration that invites three people to the front of the room and explains that they have all been hired to serve on the local fire department. Each is given a specific job. The first person is assigned the task of driving the truck. The second person is responsible for properly connecting the firehose. The third person is assigned the job of directing the firehose nozzle at the base of the fire. After explaining to each participant his or her responsibility, the preacher looks at each individually and asks, "What's your job?" to which each dutifully responds, in turn, "Drive the truck," "Hook up the hose," and "Direct the hose at the fire." Shaking his head no, the preacher explains, "You're all wrong. Your job is to put out the fire!"

When we fail to help others in our organization, and members on our own team, we neglect our primary job. Sometimes we get so bogged down in the details and the minutia, and in our own specific tasks, that we lose sight of the bigger picture. Perhaps you've worked with someone who has forgotten that his or her role serves the organization and not vice versa. Perhaps you've fallen victim to advancing your own agenda and your own interests against the goals of the organization. Whether you are a Moses in the lead seat or an Aaron or Hur who serves alongside the leader, you are called to be a team member who serves well. Each has a specific role in which to function for the common good, a point which the apostle Paul stressed to the church at Corinth when he reminded his readers that they were like one body with many parts, each serving a specific yet vitally-important function in order to complete that one body for a specific task (1 Cor. 12:12).

Moses and Jethro

"At that time I said to you, "I am not able to bear you by myself"(Deut. 1:9).

God has called you to a task that you cannot complete alone. Whether it is to lead a church or a department or a ministry, it is bigger than just you. Moses learned this lesson the hard way and wearied himself out. Great teams share the load so that no one on the team breaks. Together, they accomplish what the leader could not otherwise accomplish alone. It is oftentimes pride that drives people to productivity apart from the context of teams. They want the glory, they want their names in lights, undiluted by any additions or the sharing of credit.

Moses' father-in-law noticed the pressure that Moses was trying to bear and said,

> "What is this that you are doing for the people? Why do you sit alone? . . . What you are doing is not good. You and the people with you will certainly wear yourselves out, for the thing is too heavy for you. You are not able to do it alone" (Exod. 18:14-18).

Sometimes the people in our lives expose our inabilities. They point out either something wrong that we're doing (Matt. 18:15) or how we're doing something wrong (Exod. 18:13). Without these people in your life, you are likely either to burn out or to spin your proverbial wheels without much traction. What you are doing may seem good to you, even if it is not. Jethro pointed out, "the method can't be right if it results in everyone's frustration and exhaustion."[1] When was the last time you looked at the people on your team and saw frustration and exhaustion? What if you were part of the problem? How could you be part of the cure?

There is an unfortunate tendency in people—especially inherent in leaders—to want to operate alone. Some desire to have all of the credit so they take on all of the work. Others are afraid to delegate for fear of someone messing up a project, or they simply believe they could do better themselves. Still others simply don't want to be known by others.

Here is the poignant account of one of America's great evangelical preachers of the twentieth century that speaks volumes.

> "From the time of his conversion in 1915 and his calling to preach in 1916, A. W. Tozer continually found himself surrounded by people. Nevertheless, this man who was raised in a large and extended family, married a godly woman who brought seven children into the world, and who lived most of his adult life preaching to large gatherings of people, confided to a friend in the 1950s: 'I've had a lonely life.' Never one to use words carelessly, Tozer revealed this deep sadness during one of the few times he opened his most inmost being to anyone. But what an irony that Mr. Tozer

---

[1] Stuart, *Exodus*, Vol. 2, 416.

lived a lonely life. He had a devoted wife and lovely children, all of whom would have treasured more personal intimacy. And among those throngs of listeners to his sermons, and many of the faithful members of the four churches he pastored, many would have stood in long lines for hours just to have a few minutes of personal time and intimate two-way sharing with the man who helped them know God, but refused to let them know him.[1]

Tozer offers us a sad example of someone refusing to be known by others who could minister to us and be used by God in our growth. A more positive example, however, is found in the legendary relationship between famed authors J. R. R. Tolkien and C. S. Lewis:

> "Tolkien had drawn the curtains aside from his private inner self and invited Lewis into his sanctum. It was a personal and professional risk for the older man. Lewis could not have known it, but at this point Tolkien needed a 'critical friend,' a mentor who would encourage and criticize, affirm and improve, his writing—above all, someone who would force him to bring it to completion."[2]

---

[1] Dorsett, *A Passion For God: The Spiritual Journey of A. W. Tozer*, 16-17. (The quote is footnoted in the book as coming from an interview of James F. Hay, Sr. by D. Shepson, October 10, 1995).

[2] McGrath, *C. S. Lewis: A Life*, 129.

Tolkien and Lewis' friendship is known especially in Christian circles, and beyond, as one that produced some of the greatest Christian literature in history.

Returning now to our character study of Moses. Not only did Jethro point out what Moses was doing inefficiently (anyone can do that) he offered a better way. A way that would relieve Moses of some pressure, enlist the participation of others, and accomplish even more than Moses could have accomplished by himself. Jethro taught Moses how to delegate. Great teams distribute pressure where poor teams multiply pressure. Great teams offer ideas that are accompanied by willing hands rather than merely criticizing the work being done.

What kind of team are you on? What kind of team member are you? Do you relieve or create pressure for those you work with? Do you delegate authority to others, grant them an opportunity to succeed, and then celebrate their victories publicly, or do you cling to unmitigated control in order to take all the credit in the end? "If you do this, God will direct you, you will be able to endure, and all this people also will go to their place in peace" (Exod. 18:23).

Moses and Joshua

Moses and Joshua share a partnership that models leadership development and teamwork. In Exodus 24 and 32 we see that Joshua is with Moses during the seminal moments in the life of the people of Israel. Joshua was known as "Moses' assistant." When God called Moses to go to the mountain, he didn't have to look very far for Joshua. Moses had invested in Joshua, given him access and authority, and developed him to be an effective leader.

Great leaders produce great leaders. They not only teach them, but they allow them to take risks and reap rewards. When Amalek came to battle Israel in Exodus 17, Moses said to Joshua, "Choose for us men, and go out and fight with Amalek. Tomorrow I will stand on the top of the hill with the staff of God in my hand" (Exod. 17:9). Moses gave Joshua the authority to choose the men and the charge to go into the valley and fight.

Moses displayed confidence in Joshua. Every team, whether it is a team of two or two-hundred, must build a culture of trust. If you are the leader of the team, you have to be willing to trust your team to do what you need them to do. If you are a member on the team you must be trustworthy so that you can be entrusted. Moses entrusted the future of Israel—an entire nation of people!—to Joshua. He trusted him. Again, in Numbers 13, we see Moses send Joshua—then known as Hoshea (vs. 16)—along with a group of men to spy out the land Canaan. Moses trusted these men.

Have you developed a culture on your team where Moses can hand things off to Joshua? Can the Worship Pastor sit in the congregation one Sunday while the team he has trained up leads the charge? Can the primary Community Group teacher give new leaders the opportunity to lead? Or are people afraid that if they are not leading all the time they are losing ground? That is not leadership at all; and it is certainly not healthy teamwork.

Moses knew that his days were numbered. So too are yours. There will be a day when, as God said of Moses, he will say of you, "my servant is dead" (Josh 1:1). Will your team be ready to move forward without you? Will they be prepared to not only keep moving, but improve? It's not just you, it's "you *and . . .*"

"And Joshua the son of Nun was full of the spirit of wisdom, for Moses had laid his hands on him" (Deut. 34:9).

Team Discussion Questions

1. What was one key principle about teamwork that you learned or were reminded of in this chapter?

2. Which of the three teamwork examples (Moses and Aaron, Moses and Jethro, or Moses and Joshua) resonates most deeply with your current experience of teamwork? Why?

3. If you could grasp one lesson from this chapter and teach it to a team of people, what lesson would you choose?

FOUR

How Deborah, David, and Nehemiah Call Us to Teamwork

"That the leaders took the lead in Israel, that the people offered themselves willingly, bless the LORD!" (Judges 5:2).

This is one of my favorite verses in the Bible. As a youth pastor, every year our team would host a Volunteer Dinner, which celebrated the sacrificial work of those who served in our ministry, even if only for a short time. In fact, we invited everyone from those one-time volunteers to folks who regularly contributed their time on a weekly basis. And, to top it off, we did not ask for any commitment for future service; instead, we simply said, "Thank you!" Celebrating the impact of their service, recognizing the fruit of their effort, and thinking biblically about how we out to thank God for such volunteers, we took this evening as an opportunity to imitate Deborah's Godward praise.

Deborah's Thanksgiving (Judges 5)

Let's embark on a little thought experiment. Who is the best volunteer you know? Someone undoubtedly comes to mind. Every time you see them, they're always seemingly helping someone, or they are doing something in preparation for the next event. They are incredible gifts from God. One of the best volunteers I know is a man named Karsten. When I first arrived as the new youth pastor, Karsten approached me in his wheelchair and introduced himself. From that moment, there was not a time when Karsten was not at my side asking me how he could be of assistance. Indeed, there was hardly a single event over the next six years for which Karsten didn't volunteer on some level.

My personal favorite memory was middle school camp. We would take kids on a week-long mission camp where they would spend a few hours each day volunteering at a local organization, usually pulling weeds and tending to the landscape. And Karsten was not about to watch idly as the children worked. Oh no. Karsten was always found right in the thick of things with the kids. Not sitting in his wheelchair telling the kids which weeds to pull, but on the ground, in the dirt, elbow to elbow with the kids—laughing with the kids who were too afraid or too cool to get dirty themselves. He loved every minute of it. And his selfless service speaks volumes. Volunteers point us to Jesus as they offer themselves willingly. They tangibly display the generosity of God as they come in after a long work-week to teach a class or lead a game or offer insight into the committee meeting. They are gifts for which we ought to thank God. That's exactly what Deborah does in Judges 5.

Old Testament commentators Keil and Delitzch explain that Deborah's words in Judges 5

> "transport us in the most striking manner into the time of the judges, when Israel had no king who could summon the nation to war, but everything depended upon the voluntary rising of the strong and the will of the nation at large. The manifestation of this strength and willingness Deborah praises as a gracious gift of the Lord."[1]

Everything depended on the voluntary service of the people. If you're part of a ministry or non-profit team, the chances are that more than you imagine depends on volunteers.

Can you imagine, for one moment, where your organization would be without volunteers? What bills wouldn't get paid? What paperwork would be stacked on your desk? What classes would you still be teaching yourself, or would you still be searching for someone to lead? What soundboards would be left unbalanced? What stages would need to be set up? What phone calls would remain unmade? Can you imagine?

---

[1] Keil and Delitzsch, *Commentary on the Old Testament*, Vol. 2, 224.

If you are paid to be part of the team you serve on, when was the last time you blessed the LORD for volunteers? When was the last time you, like Paul the apostle, not only blessed God but told the volunteers that you blessed God for them? Grab a pen right now and send a quick hand-written note or grab your phone and send that text. It's as simple as that—and it will certainly go a long way.

Thanksgiving for others is an attitude that can be a game-changer for teams. We've all been discouraged by the feeling of being taken for granted. It's disheartening and deflating to believe that you are not appreciated. You begin to doubt whether or not it's worth the effort of coming in. We begin to look back on all that we've done and become resentful. As Dr. Jay Strack says, "we need to put some gratitude in our attitude." Hopefully you've been part of a team in which the leader thoroughly expressed their gratitude for you. Even if you have not, how can you begin to inject gratitude into the team culture?

David's Mighty Men (2 Samuel 23)

One of the stunning realities of Scripture is how it balances between sweeping statements that span entire nations of people and sentences when individuals are named. The biblical authors go to great lengths to help us see the width of the movement as well as its specificity.

In 2 Samuel 23, over 30 individuals are named in an extensive list of those who helped David. Each one held a particular contribution. Each was a key part to the puzzle, without whom David would have fallen. David's unparalleled success was the result not only of his relationship with the Lord, but also of his valiant soldiers' efforts. [1]

If you were to sit down and list by name the people who helped you today, how long would your list be? What if you enlarged it to include the week, month, or year? We normally don't keep such a list, but we are glad for their help nonetheless. Yes, we may say thank you in the moment, but after a while we simply forget. Don't we?

But what if you remembered? What if you sat down and wrote some thank you cards to the "mighty men" (and women) who helped you succeed along the way? What are the moments that God brings to mind when you think about such an exercise?

Let me lead the way and share some myself:

- I think of Dick AtLee who invested in me as a teenager and college student despite my giving him more than enough reasons to stop.
- I think of Thurman Hayes who led Bethel Baptist to hire me as a young youth pastor.
- I think of Doug Echols who later led Bethel to fully support sending me—and a team—to plant Catalyst Church.

---

[1] Bergen, *1, 2 Samuel*, Vol. 7, 468.

- I think of our state convention workers who rallied around Catalyst Church from the beginning.
- I think of Greg Smith and James Blackwell who helped build the stage we used for the first two years of Catalyst (including the baptismal that we built on Saturday, loaded into the trailer at midnight, and used on Sunday morning)!
- I think of the families who have given time and money and energy to help make Catalyst Church all that it is.

David's nephew Joab understood the importance of teamwork as he rallied his troops in their fight against the Syrians. And he said,

> "If the Syrians are too strong for me, then you shall help me, but if the Ammonites are too strong for you, then I will come and help you. [12] Be of good courage, and let us be courageous for our people, and for the cities of our God, and may the LORD do what seems good to him" (2 Sam. 10:11-12).

Undoubtedly Joab looked back on that day and remembered well how his team had come together.

When we thank those who have helped us along the way, we are recognizing them as gifts from God. That's why a thankless Christian is such a sad site. They have become blind to the good gifts that God has given them. Gifts which are meant to point them back to God as the giver. May it not be so for you.

Nehemiah

Nehemiah is one of the most go-to books in the Bible for leadership and teamwork. His recognition of a problem and pursuit of a solution are exemplary in many ways. And while many books on leadership and teamwork have been written solely on this book of the Bible, we will limit ourselves to a few paragraphs here.

As you read through Nehemiah 3, you are repeatedly confronted with the phrase "next to them." As in, "so and so was working and *next to them* was . . ." It is an unavoidable picture of teamwork. When you look around your team, who do you see next to you? Who do you see next to them?

Every Sunday morning I can look around at our church and see "so and so working and *next to them* . . ." I see Caleb and Austin setting up the pipe and drape and *next to them* Josh and John and Steve are putting the stage together. And *next to them* Keenan and Josh are pulling out cables for the worship team. And *next to them* Rian and Mark and Kurtis and Alan are getting the Audio and Video equipment ready. And *next to them* Sam and Sarah are getting coffee prepared. And *next to them* the hospitality team is hard at work as Kathy and Laura and Theresa are slicing fruit. And *next to them* the kids ministry team. And *next to them* . . . and on and on and on it goes.

But it's easy to stop noticing these things. It's easy to get wrapped up in the rush of the moment and to fail to see all the service and volunteering that is happening all around. It's easy to get frustrated by something small and, rather than seeing the beauty of teamwork, you find yourself complaining about a multitude of problems—or what seems to you to be problems. How sad when we turn one of the blessings God has given us into a cause for complaint.

Nehemiah had a vision of a rebuilt wall and a reestablished city. And he knew that it was going to take more than just him to accomplish this vision. So he rallied the troops and he worked for unity. It wasn't an easy task, but it was a necessary one. If your team is going to accomplish the vision it is meant to accomplish, it's going to take work. Andy Stanley recognizes, "Visions thrive in an environment of unity. They die in an environment of disunity."[1] So which are you working for? Are you known as a person working for unity? Or are you sowing seeds of disunity? Are you encouraging the other people on the team or are you griping about them and continually negating their contributions? If our teams are going to pursue the goal of the glory of God, we've got to be intentional about pursuing unity and working together.

The historical narratives in the Bible are not written in a topical form. But, like any great biography, we find a multitude of topics throughout. Teamwork is one of the many topics God

---

[1] Stanley, *Visioneering*, 168.

has woven into the history of his people. It is one of the many threads we see working for the good of his people and the glory of his name. It is a thread that he highlights in the story of his people and one which we ought to celebrate in our own lives. Truly, teamwork is a gift from God.

Team Discussion Questions

1. Who is one team member (past or present) that you are deeply thankful for?

2. Do you find it naturally easy or difficult to express thanksgiving? (You may want to take a moment now to send an encouraging text or email thanking someone)!

3. Why do you think God chose to operate through teams throughout the history of his people?

4. What is one way that you can be a better teammate because of what you learned in this chapter?

FIVE

The Wisdom of Teamwork

"What? You too? I thought I was the only one."

—C. S. Lewis[1]

Ignorance is not bliss. That misguided idea has led many astray and has been the excuse of many who simply did not want to acknowledge reality. Ignorance embraced is peril in potential. Wisdom is what we need. Biblical wisdom is what the Christian must pursue. Tommy Nelson was right in titling his study on the biblical wisdom book Ecclesiastes, *A Life Well Lived*. Without biblical wisdom life will not be well lived. It will be wasted. Without biblical wisdom teamwork will not be well lived either.

From the beginning, the wisdom of God advised man that it is not good that man should be alone. As we study the wisdom literature of the Old Testament we see this continued. We see in the pages of Scripture a calling to cooperate, and to do so wisely. But how? And why?

---

[1] Lewis, *The Four Loves*, 96.

Why do you think teamwork is wise? What have been the benefits of forsaking isolation and instead doing ministry in the context of a team? Perhaps you have seen new ideas emerge from good discussion with others. Or you've sat at the table with someone who had expertise that complimented your own. Maybe you've worked with someone who was able to get things done that you couldn't otherwise get done. But is this it? Is teamwork suggested in the wisdom of God simply because it produces better results? Or is there more?

Teamwork is wise not merely because it produces a better result, but because it reflects the heart and nature of God. Wisdom, even in the topic of teamwork, begins with God. Wise teamwork flows from the nature of the all-wise God.

Four Benefits of Teamwork

"Two are better than one, because they have a good reward for their toil. [10] For if they fall, one will lift up his fellow. But woe to him who is alone when he falls and has not another to lift him up! [11] Again, if two lie together, they keep warm, but how can one keep warm alone? [12] And though a man might prevail against one who is alone, two will withstand him—a threefold cord is not quickly broken" (Eccl. 4:9-12).

Duane Garrett, Professor of Old Testament Interpretation, points out four benefits of teamwork in his commentary on the book of Ecclesiastes.[1]

(1.) *Increased profit.* It is no mystery that two can produce more than one. Two people are likely to produce twice as much as one person. One horse by itself is suggested to pull 9,000 pounds of weight. Two horses pulling together are suggested to pull 35,000 pounds of weight!

Solomon, in Ecclesiastes 4:9, calls the product of teamwork a "good reward." Scholars Keil and Delitzsch point out,

> "The good reward consists in this, that each one of the two has the pleasant consciousness of doing good to the other by his labor, and especially of being helpful to him. In this latter general sense is grounded the idea of the reward of faithful fellowship."[2]

(2.) *Help in time of need.* Not only do we see the benefit of increased profit in teamwork, but we find help in time of need. Every person in ministry has, at one point or another, found oneself looking at a situation and saying, "I don't know what to do." Or perhaps worse, "I know the right thing to do, but I don't know if I can do it!" Ministry is difficult. Sometimes it is plain

---

[1] Garrett, *Proverbs, Ecclesiastes, Song of Songs*, Vol. 14, 308.
[2] Keil and Delitzsch, *Commentary on the Old Testament*, Vol. 6, 698.

hard work that feels overwhelming and indeed is overwhelming. In these moments we see the blessings of teamwork.

We need someone to "lift us up" (Eccl. 4:10) in the crushing moments of leadership and ministry. We need someone who will help us stand and encourage us to speak when the situation calls for it; we need someone who will help us in our time of need. Teamwork is the constant reminder that we are not alone, that we have help.

(3.) *Emotional comfort.* In verse 11, Solomon illustrates two friends who are found sleeping unprotected from the elements and are forced to rely on each other for warmth. The illustration is believed to point out the emotional comfort that teamwork provides. It is an illustration that C. S. Lewis understood when he defined friendship as the moment in which we look at another person and say, "What? You too? I thought I was the only one!"[1]

When was the last time you looked at someone on your team and knew that you were not alone in ministry? When was the last time that you had to make a difficult decision, and knowing that you were not making it alone was one of the strengthening realities that helped you up? God is so gracious in giving us teams with which to serve!

(4.) *Protection.* Finally, Solomon points out the protection that teamwork brings. In case you haven't noticed, we have an

---

[1] Lewis, 96.

enemy. We have one who seeks to devour us and destroy us and tempts us with lies that echo in our minds and hearts. He wants so badly to see our ruin.

God, in his kindness, has given us teams as a weapon against this enemy. When he attacks one, the others may rise to fight. He who might prevail against one who is alone has a harder time when we are in the context of teams.

During our first two years of planting Catalyst Church, there were a handful of situations that I looked back on and said, "I'd have quit if I were in this alone." Just a few months after launching our public services the husband and father of one of our beginning families passed away unexpectedly. There is no doubt in my mind that had our church not functioned as a team and the elders not stepped up and served, it would have crushed me emotionally. I simply could not have handled such a daunting situation alone. I still remember walking down the hospital hallway to find a quiet corner and thanking God for surrounding me with such a capable team in that moment. God knew precisely what I needed, and he delivered.

Pastor Mark Dever writes from his own personal experience, "I can honestly say that moving to a plurality of elders in our church has been the single most helpful event to me in my pastoral ministry here in Washington, D. C."[1]

No doubt there are many other benefits of teamwork. Anyone who has served with a team could add to the list. But all

---

[1] Dever, *The Deliberate Church*, 135.

too often, we fail to remember that teamwork is a gift of an all-wise God. A gift for which we ought often to give thanks.

Psalms and Proverbs

The psalms and proverbs of the Old Testament give us the songs and wisdom sayings of Israel. We know what they believed by reading what they sang and by hearing the advice they passed on from generation to generation. We see that they acknowledged community as a good gift from a benevolent God who loved them. We see that they valued even the difficult conversations they were able to have with one another as for their benefit and good. We see that they believed that a properly functioning team was beautiful, not just for the results that it produced, but that it was pleasing in the sight of God.

- "He who walks with the wise becomes wise, but the companion of fools suffers harm" (Prov. 13:20).
- "Faithful are the wounds of a friend" (Prov. 27:6).
- "As iron sharpens iron, so one man sharpens another" (Prov. 27:17).
- "Behold, how good and pleasant it is when brothers dwell in unity" (Psa. 133:1).

Christ himself dwells in the midst of our unity. Our unity is his cross becoming real in our hearts, as we demote self for his sake and exalt him more. By our unity in Christ, we are not just being nice; we are being prophetic and declarative. We are saying to all the divisive, selfish idols of this world,

> "Jesus is Lord, *and you're not*. Jesus makes life sweet, *and you don't*. Jesus brings us together, *and you can't*. You have no claim on us here. We belong to the Lord Jesus Christ, the crucified Friend of sinners, and we will have the whole world know it by our strong and joyous unity in our Savior."[1]

Teamwork, governed and guided by Scripture, is wise and pleasing to God. It is something that we ought to value as precious. It is something to be received as a gift for our good. It is a gift of grace which ought to lead us to songs of thanksgiving. Is that the case for you?

It should be. It can be.

---

[1] Hughes, *Proverbs: Wisdom that Works*, 103-04.

Team Discussion Questions

1. Why do you think teamwork is wise?

2. Which of the four benefits of teamwork listed resonates most deeply with you? Why?

3. What are the practical implications of this chapter for your team?

4. How has your experience in teamwork helped you to deepen your enjoyment of God and be a better worshipper?

SIX

Hearing the Prophetic Call to Teamwork

"The voice of your watchmen—they lift up their voice, together they sing for joy; for eye to eye they see the return of the LORD to Zion" (Isaiah 52:8).

The Prophets' primary function is to point us to Christ. By warning us of the hell-bound aim of sin, by revealing to us the magnetic beauty of the gospel, and by inviting us to turn from our sins and trust in Christ, the prophets call to us. When we think of the prophets we picture the outcast, lone ranger calling out God's people and pleading with them to return to God. We picture John the Baptist alone in the wilderness. We see Jonah single-handedly running from God and Jeremiah, known as the "Lonely Prophet."

And yet these lone rangers, and their call to repentance and faith, provide essential lessons for us to learn about teamwork. In this chapter, we will consider three:

- Sometimes you need a team to get you to move.

- Sometimes you don't have a team to work with.
- Sometimes the whole team will be wrong—even sinfully wrong.

The truth is that we experience the richness of the gospel better in the context of team than we do alone. Surely it is not good that we are alone. We need each other. Without a team we tend to drift and rarely, if ever, drift in the correct direction. We need to be aware of the benefits and burdens of teams. The prophets shake us up and point us to Christ-exalting teamwork.

Sometimes You Need a Team to Get You to Move

The point of the prophets was to call people to Jesus. The prophets heralded a message of faith and repentance, something their hearers were not producing themselves. Repentance and restoration with God. Whether by breaking the laws which God had originally given them or following the godless passions of their culture, the people to whom the prophets were sent desperately needed outside intervention.

- Edom was dependent on Obadiah's warning regarding the Day of the Lord.
- Israel was dependent on Joel's condemnation of their sins.

- Nineveh was dependent on Jonah as God's messenger of repentance and mercy.
- Joshua and the people were dependent on Haggai in moving towards rebuilding the temple.

God, in his kindness, spoke through the vessels of these men. Without the mouthpiece the message would not have been received. The gospel is good news that must be announced through human instruments, through people.

Sometimes God uses people to speak to us. They are gifts to us. We need them. Sometimes you need a team to get you to take action.

Keith and I would periodically sit down and dream about future ministry endeavors. I would talk about the book I was going to write . . . one day. And he would talk about the time that he was going to carve out in order to compose music . . . one day. Eventually we looked at each other and said, "Enough talking about 'one day'." We encouraged each other to take steps in the right direction in order to achieve our goals. I began writing, and he began composing. Eventually Keith went on to sign a contract with Red Tie Music as a composer. And, needless to say, you're holding in your hands the fruit of Keith's provoking questions to me about actually writing a book. Who is it that has prompted you into action?

The prophets often called God's people to move from sin and towards righteousness. Unapologetically they called God's people to repentance. In 2 Samuel 12, God uses the prophet

Nathan to call King David to repentance. It wasn't until David was confronted by his sin through another person that he was moved to repentance. We all need a Nathan who will call us to repentance. Billy Graham pointed this out as he commented on his friendship with multiple U. S. Presidents,

> "Every president needs some people around him who still call him by his first name and tell him exactly what they think . . . He becomes isolated partially because even his friends are afraid to tell him the truth. Everybody needs some friends around him who will just say, 'You are *wrong!*' And that includes me."[1]

Graham not only recognized his need for men who would surround him and hold him accountable, he practiced it.

> "Perhaps the greatest safeguard was another lesson he took from the Gospels. Graham had his band of disciples, a small group of lifelong friends, like Grady Wilson and Cliff Barrows, and Bev Shea, who remained at his side, kept him humble and honest, played practical jokes, teased him, trusted him, and in Shea's case was still living in a house just down the mountain in Montreat when he was ninety-seven years old. Wilson especially was clear about his calling in life: 'If

---

[1] Gibbs and Duffy, *The Preacher and The Presidents*, xii.

the Lord keeps Billy anointed,' he liked to say, 'I'll keep him humble'."[1]

Sometimes you need a team to get you to move. You need outside engagement calling you to take a step in the right direction. Sometimes you need a team to intervene and rebuke you for continually moving in the wrong direction. Each prophet stands as a reminder to us that sometimes God calls us to be the voice for another and sometimes he uses the voice of another in calling to us.

Unfortunately we have a tendency in the modern church to deny our need for God to speak through others. In our love for autonomy and individualism, we don't want them to see our faults or to speak truth into our lives. The thought of someone speaking to us in any sort of prophetic way sends us outside of our comfort zone. God may "speak to us" during our quiet time or every once in a while through a sermon. But could he actually speak to us through other believers who bear his revealed Word to us? Pastor and author J. D. Greear challenges us to reconsider,

> "When you gather with your church or your small group, do you do so with the expectation that God may have words—gospel promises, warnings, and exhortations for you to give others in the church, or that he may have such words for others to give to you?

---

[1] *Ibid.*, 51.

Do you come ready to speak in the Spirit and listen for the Spirit? [...] You see, God intends *all* of us to be his vessels in the church, not just pastors and leaders."[1]

Sometimes you need a team to get you to move.

Sometimes You Don't Have a Team

Jeremiah, as previously noted, is referred to as "The Lonely Prophet." Coming from a family of priests that had been dismissed from their priestly duties, called to be a bachelor in a culture that had no word for or understanding of bachelorhood, Jeremiah embodied loneliness.

Jeremiah, and each of the prophets as they stood by themselves, remind us that we do not always have a team with which to work. Sometimes we have a burden, a sense of calling, and a dream . . . and no support.

Church planters, as they begin their journey, are encouraged to focus on their calling from God in planting a church. This is such a point of emphasis because there will be days in which absolutely everything is considered a waste and they will doubt absolutely everything. Every crutch they have leaned on will be kicked out and every supportive voice will sound critical. And on those days, they must stand on the rock of God's calling on their lives.

---

[1] Greear, *Jesus Continued: Why the Spirit Inside You is Better Than Jesus Beside You,* 148.

When Jeremiah experienced the shaking loneliness of his call, he would mentally replay those words in his head, "Before I formed you in the womb, I knew you" (Jer. 1:5). Sometimes you do not have a team to work with. Sometimes the call is lonely. Sometimes we are all too familiar with the words of dejected Elijah, "I am the only one left" (1 Kgs. 19:10).

We would do well to remember the words of the Psalmist who wrote, "God settles the solitary in a home; he leads out the prisoners to prosperity, but the rebellious dwell in a parched land" (Psa. 68:6). He settles the solitary in a home. Other translations have it, "he puts the lonely in a family."[1] And how does he do this? Through the isolation, the forsaking of his own Son. The loneliest person in the Bible is Jesus. The loneliest moment recorded in the Bible is when Jesus cried out to his Father, "My God, My God, why have you forsaken me?" (Matt. 27:46; Mark 15:35). And for the first time, his Father was silent. Jesus was all alone.

And because Christ was forsaken, we are accepted. Because he was counted as a stranger, we are counted as sons and daughters. God truly has put the lonely in a family.

---

[1] See NIV, NLT, ISV, and NAS among other translations.

Sometimes the Whole Team can be Wrong—Even Sinfully Wrong.

In Ezekiel 34, God calls out the shepherds of Israel for their sinful failures in leading his people. What's telling, for our purposes, is that he called out the shepherds—plural. That's more than one. That's a team. And this team was dead wrong.

> "The word of the Lord came to me: [2] Son of man, prophesy against the shepherds of Israel; prophesy and say to them: 'This is what the Sovereign Lord says: Woe to you shepherds of Israel who only take care of yourselves! Should not shepherds take care of the flock? [3] You eat the curds, clothe yourselves with the wool and slaughter the choice animals, but you do not take care of the flock. [4] You have not strengthened the weak or healed the sick or bound up the injured. You have not brought back the strays or searched for the lost. You have ruled them harshly and brutally. [5] So they were scattered because there was no shepherd, and when they were scattered they became food for all the wild animals. [6] My sheep wandered over all the mountains and on every high hill. They were scattered over the whole earth, and no one searched or looked for them'."

Ezekiel exposes a team that was wrong. Sinfully wrong. They had fed their own passions and appetites at the expense of the people they were called to protect and feed. They had ignored the needs of those under their leadership while making sure their own needs were more than met.

The dangers of leaders who refuse to surround themselves with a team are plentiful. But just because a team is in agreement does not mean that they are right. Teams can be wrong. They can fail to move quickly when urgency is required. They can refuse to make the difficult call in hopes of avoiding difficult conversations. They can fail to confront the sin among each other. In 2011 the Pennsylvania State University football program was faced with a crisis as Jerry Sandusky, a long-time assistant coach, was indicted for 45 counts of sexual abuse to minors. The situation degenerated from there when it was revealed that his boss, head coach Joe Paterno, had some previous knowledge of Sandusky's hidden sin, but failed to take the action that was expected from such a well-respected member of the community. The bottom line is that when the team fails, people suffer.

- "Rebels and sinners shall be broken together" (Isa. 1:28).
- "both of them shall burn together" (Isa. 1:31).
- "Take counsel together, but it will come to nothing" (Isa. 8:10).
- "Manasseh devours Ephraim, and Ephraim devours Manasseh, together they are against Judah" (Isa. 9:21).

Being a part of a ministry team is a gift from God. It is an entrustment of authority and influence for which each person will give an account individually. It is also a tremendous responsibility. As we serve on teams we remember that sometimes it takes a team to get you to move, and we thank God for the teams in our lives that have helped us repent and grow in our faith and take steps of obedience. As we serve on teams we remember that you don't always have a team with which to work. As we serve on teams we tread carefully and humbly as we know that sometimes teams can be wrong, even sinfully wrong.

Team Discussion Questions

1. Which of the three main points resonated most with you? Why?

2. The nature of the Prophets is that God uses others as a mouthpiece to speak to us. Who has God used recently to encourage you or to motivate you to obedience?

3. Without using names or disparaging someone's character, can you recall an experience of being part of a team that was wrong, even sinfully wrong?

SEVEN

Teamwork in the Gospels

"It is grace, nothing but grace, that we are allowed to live in community with Christian brethren."

—Dietrich Bonhoeffer[1]

"More than once Jesus said that his people would demonstrate their love for him by obeying his commandments (John 14:15, 23). And the obedience which interests him is not only individual but corporate. Together individuals in churches will go, disciple, baptize, teach to obey, love, remember, and commemorate his substitutionary death with the bread and the cup."

—Mark Dever[2]

J esus never used the word "team." Nor did he ever deliver a sermon outlining how to operate as a team or institute a team. He did not leave for posterity a book on teamwork, neither did he travel the countryside teaching the principles of teamwork. But it is unquestionable that he valued teamwork. It

---

[1] Bonhoeffer, *Life Together*, 20.
[2] Dever, *The Church*, xi.

is clear in what he says and how he acts that he expected his followers to fulfill their ministry through the concept of teamwork. You cannot obey Jesus and ignore teams. You cannot follow Jesus and forsake the call to cooperate.

Jim Putnam explains,

> "As I read the Scriptures, I see team everywhere. Teams have a common purpose; they run the same play at the same time and work together in their respective positions."[1]

Chances are you've been part of a team that made you think, "Yes! This is pleasing to God. This is how Jesus wanted us to cooperate. This is good."

In the Gospel narratives we see Jesus' value and emphasis on teamwork as he called, empowered, and sent forth the Twelve Disciples.

Jesus Called the Twelve

Why didn't Jesus simply do ministry by himself? Certainly, that would have been easier than dealing with the young and inexperienced disciples. All of the painful moments of suffering and the harmful results of others' poor decisions could have

---

[1] Putman, *Church Is a Team Sport: A Championship Strategy for Doing Ministry Together*, Kindle location 16.

been avoided if he simply did things himself. For example, he could have avoided being nagged by the mother of the sons of Zebedee (Matt. 20:20). Or, he could have finished his mid-sail nap that was interrupted by the disciples as recorded in Mark chapter 4.

But he didn't. He called Twelve to himself. He invited the lowly and nobodies—according to the standards of the world—to be part of his team. And he didn't just invite them, he summoned them. He called them. Jesus chose teamwork.

> "And he went up on the mountain and called to him those whom he desired, and they came to him. [14] And he appointed twelve (whom he also named apostles) so that they might be with him and he might send them out to preach [15] and have authority to cast out demons. [16] He appointed the twelve: Simon (to whom he gave the name Peter); [17] James the son of Zebedee and John the brother of James (to whom he gave the name Boanerges, that is, Sons of Thunder); [18] Andrew, and Philip, and Bartholomew, and Matthew, and Thomas, and James the son of Alphaeus, and Thaddaeus, and Simon the Zealot, [19] and Judas Iscariot, who betrayed him" (Mark 3:13-19).

Jesus called to himself those whom he desired. Jesus desired teamwork. What a beautiful and encouraging truth. If Jesus desired teamwork, so should we. But far too often we turn our heads to potential teammates and think, "Man, they would just slow me down. They would just mess my plan up." And yet, we see Jesus embracing people as he fulfills his mission. And not just the best people! Jesus didn't relegate his team to the best, brightest, and most significant.

Pastor and theologian John Macarthur comments on Jesus' unlikely choice to represent him and carry forth his message:

> "No backup plan, and no backup crew and a risky strategy, wouldn't you say? But these men are not the explanation for the advance of the gospel. They were available and they were empowered and the gospel went over the whole world and continues to do so as a legacy to their faithfulness. Our Lord uses ordinary, weak, failing, ignorant saints . . . guess why? That's the only kind there are. Welcome to the group."[1]

If Jesus valued teamwork, so should we. When we choose to do ministry alone we are not acting in harmony with Jesus' clear example. When we devalue the teams on which we serve—either through poor participation or through a thankless attitude—we devalue that which Jesus intentionally choose and even desired.

---

[1] MacArthur, "Twelve Ordinary Men" on Mark 3:13-19, preached on October 11, 2009.

Jesus Empowered the Twelve

This is where we get to the really intriguing part. Jesus not only choose the twelve but he empowered them to do ministry. He invested in them. Jesus entrusted his own authority to the Twelve! (Can you imagine the moments he put his head in his hands or lifted his eyes to the heavens as he watched twelve goofballs that would be this team of world-changers)?! As Paul did with the Thessalonians, Jesus shared not only his teaching but his life as well. Jesus' heart for his team of disciples is expressed in his prayer recorded in John 17.

- "Yours they were and you gave them to me" (vs. 6).
- "I have given them the words that you gave me, and they have received them and have come to know in truth that I came from you; and they have believed that you sent me" (vs. 8).
- "I am praying for them" (vs. 9).
- "All mine are yours, and yours are mine, and I am glorified in them" (vs. 10).
- "Holy Father, keep them in your name . . . that they may be one, even as we are one" (vs. 11).
- "As you sent me into the world, so I have sent them into the world" (vs. 18).

Jesus prayed in this manner because the team—his team—was precious to him. Just picture for a moment all the human experiences Jesus shared with his team: he had laughed with them, traveled with them, celebrated with them, wept with them, prayed with them, counseled them, was exhausted because of them, disagreed with them, but—he loved them. He received this team as a gift from God. "You gave them to me." This was absolutely in agreement with Mark 3 when he "called to himself those he desired." This was Jesus' team—imperfect and full of blemishes as they were.

Our participation in teams is an answer to Jesus' prayer in John 17. When we agree to cooperate and link arms to advance the gospel, we are providing a practical outworking of Jesus' prayer that we would be one. When we choose not to be part of the team, however, we are moving in the opposite direction as Jesus prayed. We are in direct opposition to the prayer of Jesus. I don't know about you, but that's the last place I want to be!

Jesus also said of the Christian team, "Whoever believes in me will also do the works that I do; and greater works than these will he do, because I am going to the Father" (John 14:12). Jesus knew that an investment in the team was necessary because he understood his time on earth with them was limited. He knew that he would not physically be present with them to advance the ministry in the future. He recognized that God had a global plan for his glory that would exceed the geographic regions Jesus would visit.

Therefore, not only did Jesus empower the Twelve, but he sent them.

Jesus Sent the Twelve

Jesus calls the disciples, empowers the disciples, and sends the disciples. The "sentness" of Jesus' disciples cannot be clearer in the Scripture. "As the father has sent me, even so I am sending you" (John 20:21).

Jesus did not just say this to one disciple, but to the eleven. And when we consider it in light of the rest of Scripture, it's clear that Jesus meant *all* believers. To be part of Jesus' team is to be sent. There is simply no getting around it. As Charles Spurgeon said, "every Christian is either a missionary or an imposter."[1]

In Mark 9 Jesus said to his disciples, "The harvest is plentiful, but the laborers are few; therefore pray earnestly to the Lord of the harvest to send out laborers into his harvest" (Mark 9:37-38). Notice that Jesus did not call his disciples to merely hope for one good laborer. He called them to pray for laborers, plural. Billy Graham is not the lone answer to this prayer. It will take many. It will take Billy Graham and Luis Palau and stadium preachers. And it will take pastors and preachers who serve in the local church week in and week out. And it will take men and women who volunteer on youth committees and church plant set-up teams and ministry advisory boards and worship teams. And it will take missionaries who live and serve in difficult places where their names cannot be published for fear of persecution. It will take

---

[1] Spurgeon, *The Sword and the Trowel* (1873), 127.

women serving among college students in Vietnam and in the mountains of Afghanistan and in the inner cities of North America. It will take men leading their families and sitting in the marketplaces of closed countries and leading ministries in El Salvador. It will take a team.

Jesus valued team as he called, empowered, and sent the Twelve. As you look back on your experience on teams, who is it that invited you to be part of the team? Who is it that invested in you and empowered you to be a contributing member of the team? Who is it that sent you into that new area or position of influence? Jesus calls you to cooperate as a contributing team member.

The Power of "With"

I'm becoming more and more convinced that two of the most important words spoken in the context of team (and particularly the church), are "with me." It's a gift of grace to have a friendly person say, "Would you like to sit *with me*?" Or to be invited to serve on a team, "*with me*." A brief overview of the life of Christ shows us this:

- "And he shall be called Emmanuel (which means God *with* us)" (Matt 1:23).
- "And he appointed twelve (whom he also named apostles) so that they might be *with* him and he might send them out to preach" (Mark 3:14).

- "And he called to him the crowd *with* his disciples and said to them, "if anyone would come after me, let him deny himself and take up his cross and follow me" (Mark 8:34).

- "And after six days Jesus took *with* him Peter and James, and John his brother, and led them up a high mountain by themselves. (Where they would hear God's thundering approval of Jesus, His Son)" (Matt. 17:1).

- "Jesus said, 'I will keep the Passover at your house *with* my disciples'" (Matt 26:18).

- "Then Jesus went *with* them (disciples) to a place called Gethsemane" (Matt 26:36).

- "And behold, I am *with* you always, to the end of the age" (Matt 28:20).

There is no room for the lone ranger among those who are following Jesus. Just as he was with his disciples so we are called to be with one another. This is the beauty of team. Imitating Jesus as we labor—and often struggle—alongside each other. Dealing with quirks and personalities and frustrations and the multiplied results of a group of people. This is where Jesus chose to operate, in team.

When the Team Breaks Down

Teamwork among Christians is not without its difficulties. We do not always see eye to eye. Even when we agree on theological foundations, and each point to the same Bible, we do not always arrive at the same conclusions and agree on how things should be accomplished. And sometimes we are hurt, even offended, by others. Just a surface level reading of the Gospels familiarizes you with the relational fractions the disciples experienced. They were prideful, arrogant, degrading at times, foolish at others.

Successful and God-honoring teamwork is contingent on our laying down our rights and pursuing reconciliation. Four principles of reconciliation are laid out in Matthew 18:

BE AWARE OF THE PREVENTATIVES OF RECONCILIATION (MATT. 18:1-9)

Jesus calls us to be aware of everything that might prevent us from reconciling with others. Here he points out the attitude of pride and the presence of personal sin. Pride prevents us from reconciling with others as we think too highly of ourselves and too little of others. There is no place for pride in the kingdom. Personal sin keeps us from reconciliation when we are fearful that our sin might be exposed. Rather than running that risk, we choose to keep pointing fingers. What in your life is a preventing reconciliation?

See God's Pursuit in Reconciliation
(Matt. 18:10-14)

You simply cannot get to know God without getting to know his heart for reconciliation. This is his desire, his will. He does not want even one little lamb to perish. Shouldn't we who are his children be the same?

Be a Community of Reconciliation
(Matt. 18:15-20)

In a passage known as a commentary on church discipline, Jesus teaches us that his church will be a community of reconciliation. Isn't it sad when a church is known for division more than for reconciliation? However, an organization, whether a church or a ministry or a school, will never be known for reconciliation if it's ministry and leadership teams are not known for reconciliation.

Be an Individual of Reconciliation
(Matt. 18:21-35)

Finally, in a pointed conversation with Peter Jesus calls each of us to be reconciling individuals. Have you ever met someone who complained that their church wasn't welcoming to new-comers, but in reality it was that individual themselves who wasn't welcoming to individuals? That's what's going on here. Jesus is looking at Peter and saying, "I'm not just giving you a theory that is a good idea for the church at large, I'm telling you what you must be."

Jesus valued teamwork. If we are to follow him, we must value it as well. And we must work diligently to remove every obstacle to God-honoring teamwork. Especially those we find in our own hearts.

Team Discussion Questions

1. What key principles about teamwork stood out to you from this chapter?

2. In what ways have you seen the lessons of this chapter worked out in your current team experience?

3. If you are a team leader, how did this chapter challenge you in your leadership?

4. If you are not the leader, how did this chapter challenge you in your role?

5. How important is it to a team to handle conflict well? What principles in this section resonated with you?

EIGHT

The Acts of Teamwork

"The goal of the church is never for one person to be equipped and empowered to lead as many people as possible to Christ. The goal is always for all of God's people to be equipped and empowered to lead as many people as possible to Christ."

—David Platt[1]

There are certain times and places in which we wonder what it would be like to be a fly on the wall. To observe how people interacted and disagreed. To see decisions being made and implemented. The young politician may daydream about congressional conversations. An aspiring author wants to know what his or her hero's writing nook looks like. The historian imagines what it was like to live and breathe in a past day and age.

For the twenty-first century Christian, we do not have to imagine what it was like in the early church. God has given us a sufficient glimpse through Luke's recording in the book of Acts. Now, if you have read the book you know that there is plenty

---

[1] Platt, *Radical Together*, 57.

left to wonder about and imagine. For instance, what was it like to hear and feel the Spirit move in like a mighty rushing wind in Acts 2? What did Peter's face look like when God told him to take the gospel message to the Gentiles? How scared was Ananias when God told him to embrace the known persecutor Saul as a brother in Christ? How did the Holy Spirit point out Paul and Barnabas to the congregation in Acts 13? These and other questions naturally arise as we read. But this in no way diminishes the book's competence in informing and instructing us as modern believers. We have a sufficient Word.

Throughout the book of Acts we see the people of God operating in and through communities. In Acts 2:42-47 we see the community gathered together and exemplifying healthy biblical community. In Acts 4:32 we see the community living both sacrificially and generously. In Acts 6 and 7 we see the community serving. In Acts 13 we see the community sending as the church in Antioch commissions Paul and Barnabas. And in Acts 20 we see Paul and the community of Ephesian elders weeping together at the likely end of their earthly fellowship.

These are glimpses of the church acting as a team on a mission. Granted, it was not without its own hiccups or frustrations. We see Ananias and Sapphira flat out lie about their generosity. We see the apostles disagree at times. We even see Luke and others try to prevent the apostle Paul from going where he felt led to go. And yet the early church gives us some principles of teamwork that we would do well to remember as modern believers.

Teamwork thrives when we sacrifice for one another and when we send one another. Essentially, teamwork thrives when the team comes together around, and is motivated by, the gospel.

Teamwork Thrives When We Sacrifice for One Another

The early church displayed the sacrificial nature of the gospel-centered life as they cared for one another. The examples in the book of Acts are not of men and women merely being considerate but of sacrificial generosity based on the sacrificial generosity they've received from Jesus. J. D. Greear explains, "The clearest mark of God's grace in your life is a generous spirit toward others."[1] I don't know about you, but that sentence confronts me. Do I have a generous spirit towards others? Is it evidenced by a generous life?

> "And all who believed were together and had all things in common. [45] And they were selling their possessions and belongings and distributing the proceeds to all, as any had need" (Acts 2:44-45).

> "Now the full number of those who believed were of one heart and soul, and no one said that any of the

---

[1] Greear, *Gospel: Recovering the Power that Made Christianity Revolutionary*, Kindle location 122.

things that belonged to him was his own, but they had everything in common. [33] And with great power the apostles were giving their testimony to the resurrection of the Lord Jesus, and great grace was upon them all. [34] There was not a needy person among them, for as many as were owners of lands or houses sold them and brought the proceeds of what was sold [35] and laid it at the apostles' feet, and it was distributed to each as any had need. [36] Thus Joseph, who was also called by the apostles Barnabas (which means son of encouragement), a Levite, a native of Cyprus, [37] sold a field that belonged to him and brought the money and laid it at the apostles' feet" (Acts 4:32-37).

Can you remember a time when someone truly sacrificed for you? Perhaps you think of your parents who worked extra jobs or longer hours to make ends meet. You may have had a teacher who purchased supplies with their own money. (Actually, I can almost guarantee you had a teacher who did that—you just were never aware of it). Or maybe you had a friend who was an especially thoughtful gift-giver and did something special for you. One Christmas my brother-in-law Adam gave me a mason jar coffee mug. That would've been cool enough for me, but his generosity did not stop there. Instead, he also crafted a leather wrap to protect the mug, fitted it to achieve the perfect grip, wove it together seamlessly, and branded it with our church logo on it. He sacrificed the money, time, and energy to do something special.

When was the last time you sacrificed for someone else? When did you last provide a meal for a family who was in the throes of hectic season? When did you last make the financial investment in something for someone else other than for yourself? If the people on your team were to describe you, how many of them would think of a time that you were sacrificially generous towards them?

We don't like to think of people sacrificing for us. "We're not that bad off," we like to say.

George Müller, the nineteenth-century Englishman and founder of orphanages, was not a man who liked to publicly share personal needs or even specific needs of his ministry. He was afraid of taking his eyes off of God as the sole provider. While that is certainly an understandable fear—even admirable, I might add—it is also unfortunate in some ways. While Müller is exemplary in pursuing God's provision through prayer, I wonder if he missed some opportunities for God to provide in other ways. I'm reminded of the story of the man who was caught in his house as floods waters began to rise. He prayed that God would rescue him. Moments later a rescue boat came to usher the man to safety, but the man waved him off saying, "I'm waiting for God." The waters continued to rise. Another rescue boat came, and again the man said, "I'm waiting for God." Finally the man was stuck on his roof as the waters continued to rise, and a rope fell from a helicopter hovering above him. "I'm waiting for God," he shouted, and soon thereafter he drowned. When he met God, the story goes, God said, "I sent you two boats and a helicopter."

J. D. Greear explains the Reformer Martin Luther's thinking on this issue:

> "Martin Luther observed that when the Lord answers our prayer 'for daily bread,' he does so in a variety of ways. He gives the farmer the skill and ability to plant the seed, grow and harvest the grain. He equips someone to build the road on which we transport the grain, and someone who will drive the vehicle that carries it. He equips the engineer who designs the plant that processes the grain, the store owner who packages the bread for purchase, and the advertiser who alerts us to its availability. . . . Thus, God answers our prayer for daily bread by a multiplicity of vocational endowments."[1]

When the man stranded in the flood refused help, he refused God's gift. In his biography on George Müller, Arthur T. Pierson writes,

> "To impart the knowledge of affairs to so much larger a band of helpers brought in every way a greater blessing, and especially so to the helpers themselves. Their earnest, believing, importunate prayers were thus called forth, and God only knows how much the

---

[1] Greear, *Jesus Continued*, 128.

101

consequent progress of the work was due to their faith, supplication, and self-denial."[1]

The early church displayed what it means to sacrifice for one another. "They were selling their possessions and belongings and distributing the proceeds to all, as any had need" (Acts 2:45). Right there in the book of Acts is a picture of true Christian charity; there, for everyone to see, is the mark of the true Christian. John Stott points out that these offerings "were and are voluntary," and that "every Christian has to make conscientious decisions before God in this matter, we are all called to generosity." Stott summarizes, "Christian fellowship is Christian caring and Christian caring is Christian sharing."[2] We simply cannot be a part of the redeemed people of God and *not* be willing to sacrifice for one another. The apostle John would go on to tell us, "if anyone has the world's goods and sees his brother in need, yet closes his heart against him, how does God's love abide in him?" (1 John 3:17). How many times have we been on teams where we soon discovered others did not seem to share a compassion for those in need? Or, how many times have we sat through meetings absolutely clueless—and probably a bit careless as well—about the needs of others? The answer to both is probably more than it should be. "There are

---

[1] Pierson, *George Müller of Bristol*, 155.
[2] Stott, *Bible Speaks Today: The Message of Acts*, 84.

some graces and blessings that God gives only in the 'meeting together' with other believers."[1]

While your team may not seem like the appropriate place to have a conversation about sacrificial generosity, it could be the perfect place for you to *display* sacrificial generosity. This is especially true if you serve on a team with others who have not experienced the generosity of Jesus. How powerful would it be for an unbelieving teammate to observe, or be the recipient of, the extravagant love of Jesus through you?

Teamwork Thrives When We Celebrate The Sending of One Another

The gospel produces missionaries. Individuals whose hearts are gripped by the gospel become missionaries. It is here worth mentioning again Charles Spurgeon's notable quip that, "Every Christian is either a missionary or an imposter." The same must be true of Christian teams. Ministry teams gathered around the gospel must be missionary-minded ministry teams.

What place does your team have in the Great Commission? If you are part of a team in the Christian Education field, how do you see your team training up future apologists, teachers, and authors? Recently I was in Southeast Asia when one of our team members, a Neuroscience major in college, began to articulate a desire to be a missionary in the

---

[1] Whitney, *Spiritual Disciplines for the Christian Life*, 92.

scientific research community. He was beginning to see his life as a mission trip. One of the reasons that team was so successful was a common commitment to the great commission. Throughout the trip we regularly encouraged each other in our efforts to advance the gospel, and we celebrated each success. Now you need to understand that your team doesn't have to be on a foreign mission trip to embrace this mentality. How can you begin to frame your team meetings, goals, and successes in light of the great commission of making disciples of all nations? Alvin Reid keenly observed, "Life is a mission trip. Take it!" Teams that operate under the authority of Jesus, and for the glory of Jesus, are going to be about the mission of making Jesus known, whatever sphere of culture they are in.

In Acts 10, God uses Peter and Cornelius to illustrate that the gospel is for Gentiles as well as Jews. A major moment in the story of God, "everything about this event shows that God's way includes reconciliation and compassion offered to all who will respond."[1] Just a few chapters later, in Acts 15, God uses the leadership team at the church in Jerusalem to advance the gospel to the Gentiles. Before that, in Acts 13, we read how God uses the team at Antioch to set apart Paul and Barnabas and to send them out on their missionary journey. In Acts 16 God uses Luke, Timothy, and others to confirm Paul's call to take the gospel to Macedonia.

---

[1] Bock, *Baker Exegetical Commentary*, 380.

J. D. Greear has been instrumental in leading Summit Church to adopt the motto, "We send our best," as they seek to raise up and send out missionaries. Of course, that's easier said than done. It's a difficult task to send out staff members that are doing a great job. Our tendency is to keep those staff members for ourselves and not send them out, even if it is for kingdom building. But teamwork that is driven by the great commission must act differently. They must see themselves as a sending agency used by God. Helen Roseveare once reflected on the process of being sent as a missionary to the Congo and wrote, "It was not the committee, not a group of fellow-missionaries, but the Lord Himself—through them, it was true—who was sending me to Nebobongo."[1]

When we believe that the Lord is using the work of our team to advance *his* gospel, we are better able to lead with open hands. Rather than holding tightly to our teammates and resources, we are able to hold them in an open hand; trusting God to use them and us as he best sees fit.

Sacrificial generosity and a willingness to part with cherished friends are not the result of merely working well together. These are the results of a team being captivated and amazed at the gospel. This is critical in rightly understanding the early church. When the early church operated as it was meant to, it operated from a position of being gripped by the

---

[1] Roseveare, *Give Me This Mountain*, 87-88.

gospel. A. W. Tozer's illustration commenting on Acts 4:32 explains,

> "Has it ever occurred to you that one hundred pianos all tuned to the same fork are automatically tuned to each other? They are of one accord by being tuned, not to each other, but to another standard to which each one must individually bow. So one hundred worshippers met together, each one looking away to Christ, are in heart nearer to each other than they could possibly be were they to become 'unity' conscious and turn their eyes away from God to strive for closer fellowship."[1]

The early church, therefore, reminds us of the power and beauty of a team captivated by, and tuned to, the glorious gospel.

---

[1] Tozer, *The Pursuit of God*, 97.

Team Discussion Questions

1. In what ways do you see the principles of teamwork throughout the book of Acts?

2. If you could have experienced firsthand one moment of teamwork from the book of Acts, which moment would you choose? Why?

3. In what ways can you display sacrificial generosity for those around you?

4. What role does your team have in the Great Commission? How can that role be an encouragement as you serve?

NINE

Paul's Plea for Teamwork

"In God's economy, the team was and is vital to the propagation of the gospel and the multiplication of disciples, leaders, and churches."

—J. D. Payne[1]

"Christian fellowship, then, is self-sacrificing conformity to the gospel."

—D. A. Carson[2]

F ew people in the history of the world have worked harder for the advancement of the gospel than the apostle Paul. Paul made it his mission to spread the gospel, and he loved to see how God used others to advance the good news. We see Paul embracing teamwork throughout the book of Acts, and we hear the emotional pleas of a man deeply invested in teams throughout his letters.

In one of Paul's most heartfelt prayers Paul declared, "I thank my God in all my remembrance of you, always in every

---

[1] Payne, *The Barnabas Factor*, 2.
[2] *Basics for Believers: An Exposition of Philippians*, 16.

prayer of mine for you all making my prayer with joy, because of your partnership with in the gospel from the first day until now." (Phil. 1:3). This was more than a friendship; it was a partnership in the gospel. A partnership that was built on years of relational equity, sacrificial generosity, and working together.

Every letter recorded in Scripture is built on the premise of teamwork. Paul wrote to the Galatians out of a frustration with the breakdown of a team foundation—that we are saved by grace alone. Paul wrote the first letter to the church in Corinth to correct a team dysfunction and the second letter to celebrate the team they had together built. Paul wrote to the Ephesians to strengthen the depths of their love for Christ. Paul wrote to the church in Thessalonica to help them endure in suffering. And Paul wrote his pastoral epistles to help young churches and church leaders. If Paul didn't value teamwork, he would have never taken the time to write detailed instructions. "Let them figure it out on their own!" he would have rationalized. But he did value team, and so he did write.

With every verse Paul reminded his teams:

- You're not in this alone!
- I know it's difficult, but don't give up!
- I'm so proud of the work that you're doing!
- What you do matters!
- Keep growing!

Paul knew that God not only did gospel-advancing work through teams, but he did gospel-advancing work in teams. Do you realize that? God is actively at work in your teams in at least two major ways: (1.) God is using the efforts and work of your team to spread his glory to the nations; *and* (2.) God is actively working to spread his glory to the people in your teams in new ways every day. We're all part of the work and recipients of the work!

1 Corinthians 12—For the Common Good

Perhaps Paul's most stunning chapter on teamwork is the twelfth chapter in his first letter to the church in Corinth. In these thirty-one verses Paul magnifies the sovereign work of the Spirit in strategically and specifically gifting every individual in Christ for the work of advancing the gospel and the building up of the church. You have been uniquely gifted in Christ, he reminds his readers, for the common good of the team. God has gifted each one of us in Christ for all of us in Christ. You've been purposefully gifted and placed by God. And those around you have been uniquely gifted in Christ for the common good of the team!

> "Now there are varieties of gifts, but the same Spirit;
> [5] and there are varieties of service, but the same Lord;
> [6] and there are varieties of activities, but it is the same God who empowers them all in everyone. [7] To each is

given the manifestation of the Spirit for the common good" (1 Cor. 12:4-7).

In his sermon "Living in the Spirit and in the Body for the Common Good," John Piper highlights four phrases from this chapter: "to each of you is given . . . ," "Spirit," "manifestation," and "common good."

(1.) *To each of you is given*. Every believer is gifted. God has no children that he has not equipped for effective ministry. He has sovereignly and strategically gifted us. We didn't earn these talents, we didn't coincidently get a few random genes that added up—we were given these gifts.

(2.) *Spirit*. The Spirit is the one at work in us and through us. We are not simply given abilities; rather, we are given "manifestations of the Spirit." The same Spirit that was active in creation and active in raising Jesus from the dead is active in gifting you.

(3.) *Manifestation*. When you are exercising your God-given gift, whether that's managing the finances or organizing the event or teaching the lesson, you are allowing the Spirit to work through you.

(4.) *Common Good*. It is good that you exercise your gifts, not for your own glory but for the glory of God. Others benefit from God's work in you and through you. That is precisely the way it is supposed to be.

Paul was captivated by these truths. And we should be as well. When is the last time you thanked God for the way the event planner worked out all the details of the big corporate event? When is the last time you personally benefited from the financial officers in your organization? These are gifts from the Spirit that should lead us to Christ-exalting worship!

David Prior comments, "Again and again Paul is bringing the Corinthians back to the good of the community, not the personal whims of the individual."[1] Paul went to great lengths throughout his letter to the Corinthians to help them value one another and value team. Imagine how much more you would enjoy the committee meeting if you knew that everyone at the meeting was driven by the good of the community! While you don't necessarily have the power to change the attitude of everyone else on the team, you do have the power to change yours! Remember, God has gifted you for the good of the community. Now act like it!

Teamwork Builds Up the Body of Christ

I have been part of two substantial church building projects. One was the renovation of an old sanctuary that was given to the youth group. The second was a transition of our church plant from a coffee shop to an older sanctuary, which we were using but not renovating. Both of these projects made my head spin, as anyone who has ever encountered a similar situation can empathize. From interior decoration decisions to

---

[1] Prior, *The Message of 1 Corinthians*, 197.

logistical planning of people to audio-video needs and desires to lighting to seats to hospitality. Those projects were clear and powerful reminders of the importance of team. Could I have made all of the decisions? Perhaps, but not wisely. And thankfully, in each of those projects I was surrounded by a great team.

In Ephesians 4, Paul writes,

> "And he gave the apostles, the prophets, the evangelists, the shepherds and teachers, [12] to equip the saints for the work of ministry, for building up the body of Christ, [13] until we all attain to the unity of the faith and of the knowledge of the Son of God, to mature manhood, to the measure of the stature of the fullness of Christ, [14] so that we may no longer be children, tossed to and fro by the waves and carried about by every wind of doctrine, by human cunning, by craftiness in deceitful schemes."

The apostle was keenly aware that God was not simply going to use one tool or one type of person to build his church. It would instead be a tapestry that would be beautifully woven together. I think Paul left a few things off the list, though. He forgot the cooks, the set-up crew, the teller team, the hospitality team, the audio-video folks, the building maintenance people, and so on.

And I'm willing to bet that Paul knew some of those people would butt heads with each other. I wonder how often the prophets stood up to speak and made the teachers nervous.

"Good grief, what is this guy going to say that I'm going to have to explain in Sunday school this week?" Or, "Whatever is about to come out of her mouth, I'm going to have to fix through a staff-wide email later today!" I wonder if the shepherds' heart rates increased just a bit when the evangelists started inviting the masses. "Wait! We don't have the capacity to care for all those people!" I can only imagine that the apostles became frustrated with the logistical questions and concerns of the teachers and shepherds. "Just have faith, man!!!"

There are a variety of gifts and a multitude of the gifted. Each, of course, coming with his or her own particular quirks and qualifications. You were never meant to be on a team with people exactly like you. As one of my mentors once said, "If we agree on everything, one of us is unnecessary." You were meant to be a team member who helps the team grow in Christlikeness. Does that sound like you? Are the people you serve alongside more like Jesus because of the time they've spent with you? If not, what's preventing you from changing your ways before you get out of the chair you're sitting in?

The Best Teams are Bragging Teams

The best teams are bragging teams. They celebrate God's work in each other to the point of frustrating those around them. Have you ever grown weary of a leader who incessantly celebrates his or her church or team or teammates on all the social media websites, posting comments to Facebook, Twitter,

Instagram and the like? I certainly have. But one day I thought, "I wonder if what I'm really frustrated at is my own lack of celebration." And so I began celebrating our volunteers in more of a public manner. I began mentioning them by name in sermons or during particular services. At times, I would ask the entire church to show their gratitude for one of our teams. The church would erupt in clapping, shouts of thanks, and gratitude. We wanted to celebrate well. We wanted to brag on what God was doing in and through these people.

Paul knew how to celebrate his co-workers. In Philippians 2:19-30 he goes to great lengths to celebrate Timothy and Epaphroditus. Of Timothy Paul writes, "I have no one like him" (vs. 20). Of Epaphroditus Paul writes, "he risked his life to complete what was lacking in your service to me" (vs. 30). In Romans chapter 16, Paul mentions name after name after name of others with whom he had served on teams until he listed over 30 names! These men and women are recorded in Holy Scripture as celebrated examples.

At the end of Paul's letter to Timothy we see a less celebratory but equally informative illustration from Paul's life,

> "Do your best to come to me soon. [10] For Demas, in love with this present world, has deserted me and gone to Thessalonica. Crescens has gone to Galatia, Titus to Dalmatia. [11] Luke alone is with me. Get Mark and bring him with you, for he is very useful to me for ministry. [12] Tychicus I have sent to Ephesus. [13] When you come,

bring the cloak that I left with Carpus at Troas, also the
books, and above all the parchments" (2 Tim. 4:9-13).

Some of these men had left on good terms, some on bad
terms. But Paul wrote with a sense of loneliness. The sorrow
Paul expressed in their leaving matched the joy Paul felt in their
presence.

The apostle Paul displayed his love for teams in each one
of his letters. Paul's heartfelt pleas and prayers and celebrations
lead me to repent of my own failures in these areas and stir in
me a desire to move forward in Christ-exalting obedience. I can
only imagine how my teams would make much of Christ if I
were resolved to celebrate and pray the way Paul did! As you
look forward to meetings that are on your calendar and teams
that you'll be working with, how can you diligently work for the
common good? Who can you celebrate at the next team
gathering? There's absolutely no good excuse for not
celebrating someone on your team. Even if you're not the leader
and you think, "Well, it's not really my place . . . " try celebrating
the leader. It doesn't have to be over the top and certainly
shouldn't be insincere, but it should be done. Let us, like Paul,
pursue God's glory on our teams.

Team Discussion Questions

1. If you sat down with the apostle Paul today and he gave you some input about teamwork or about your current experience of teamwork, what do you think he would say? Why?

2. Jeff wrote, "Paul knew that God not only did gospel-advancing work through teams, but he did gospel-advancing work in teams." How has God used your team to help you cherish the gospel?

3. What difference does it make that you have been strategically gifted by God "for the common good?"

4. What is one key principle from this chapter that you can apply to your current team?

TEN

How the Beauty of Heaven
Calls Us to Teamwork

"When we come to know Christ it is not a table for two—we are brought into a massive dining room full of chairs for brothers and sisters."

—Dustin Willis[1]

John's Revelation closes the canon of Scripture with a captivating and compelling view into heaven. Jesus is worshipped. Satan is defeated. God's people are satisfied as God dwells with them. All is well that ends well, and here the ending is very well. Sometimes people ask me, "Why doesn't God just snap his fingers and be done with the whole bit? Why doesn't he just make the people in the foreign lands believe who are going to believe? Why do we have to go?" But aren't you glad he doesn't just snap his fingers? Aren't you glad that he uses us to accomplish his great purpose? Aren't you glad that God has chosen to use teams? I am.

[1] Willis, January 2, 2015, 10:20 p.m., Tweet.

I think back on the teams that I have worked with to advance the gospel and I am tremendously thankful! I think about the mission team I served with in Peru as an eleventh-grader, and I'm thankful. I think about the team in Honduras where we would travel hours each way into the mountains to take medical care and the love of Jesus, and I am thankful. I think about the team that I served with in my first full-time youth ministry position, and I am thankful. I think about the absolutely encouraging team that I have had the privilege of starting Catalyst Church with, and I am thankful! Each of those experiences is a gift from God. Each is a gift, which deepens my gratitude and is like fuel on the fire of my worship. Do you see your teamwork as a gift that increases worship in you and others? You should. I am so glad that God has, in his graciousness and sovereignty, delighted to use teams.

This truth causes me to repent of the times in which I begrudgingly participated in the team. It causes me to repent of the spirit of complacency or even neglect with which I treated God's gift to me in the form of teams. Who knows what lessons I missed and what joy I forfeited as I sulked through another team meeting or day dreamed in the middle of that board member's presentation.

Writing in exile, John had a sharpened appreciation for team. When this man, alone on the Greek island of Patmos, saw a community in heaven, his heart would have leapt at the chance to join with someone in song or in prayer or in praise. We would all do well to pay attention to the team lessons presented by this prisoner in solitary confinement. John's letter to revelation gives us some soul-strengthening hooks on which we should hang our thoughts about teamwork.

The Example of Others

No one can deny the power of example. When we see someone accomplish a task that we previously thought impossible, not only do we stand in awe of their achievement, we begin to broaden the horizon of our own potential. We begin to think, "Could I . . . ?" and "Would I . . . ?" and "Could God do that through me?" John Piper writes to pastors of the importance and impact of reading Christian biographies:

> "Biographies have served as much as any other human force in my life to resist the inertia of mediocrity. Without them I tend to forget what joy there is in relentless God-besotted labor and aspiration. . . . Living theology. Flawed and encouraging saints. Stories of grace. Deep inspiration. The best entertainment. Brothers, it is worthy your precious hours. Remember Hebrews 11. And read Christian biography."[1]

As God peels back the curtain and gives John this glimpse into heaven, it seems as though he wants John to be strengthened by the power of example. He wants John to see the

---

[1] Piper, *Brothers We Are Not Professionals*, 90, 96.

men and women who have paid the price, finished the race, and won the prize they pursued. He wants John to see them worshipping in heaven.

John records in Revelation 6:9-11,

> "When he opened the fifth seal, I saw under the altar the souls of those who had been slain for the word of God and for the witness they had borne. [10] They cried out with a loud voice, 'O Sovereign Lord, holy and true, how long before you will judge and avenge our blood on those who dwell on the earth?' [11] Then they were each given a white robe and told to rest a little longer, until the number of their fellow servants and their brothers should be complete, who were to be killed as they themselves had been" (Rev. 6:9-11).

Can you imagine the resolve that would've coursed through John's veins after such a sight?! What an encouragement. Those whose deaths on earth would've been interpreted by many to be horrific tragedy are seen securely placed under the very throne of God! And there finding rest!

Another example is found in Revelation 7:9-17,

> "After this I looked, and behold, a great multitude that no one could number, from every nation, from all tribes and peoples and languages, standing before the throne and before the Lamb, clothed in white robes, with palm branches in their hands, [10] and crying out with a loud voice, 'Salvation belongs to our God who

sits on the throne, and to the Lamb!' [11] And all the angels were standing around the throne and around the elders and the four living creatures, and they fell on their faces before the throne and worshiped God, [12] saying, 'Amen! Blessing and glory and wisdom and thanksgiving and honor and power and might be to our God forever and ever! Amen.'

[13] Then one of the elders addressed me, saying, 'Who are these, clothed in white robes, and from where have they come?' [14] I said to him, 'Sir, you know.' And he said to me, 'These are the ones coming out of the great tribulation. They have washed their robes and made them white in the blood of the Lamb.

[15] Therefore they are before the throne of God, and serve him day and night in his temple; and he who sits on the throne will shelter them with his presence.

[16] They shall hunger no more, neither thirst anymore; the sun shall not strike them, nor any scorching heat.

[17] For the Lamb in the midst of the throne will be their shepherd, and he will guide them to springs of living water, and God will wipe away every tear from their eyes'."

The question asked in verse 13 is an important one, "Who are these, clothed in white robes, and from where have they come?" The elder was drawing John's attention to them. (Note: It is a healthy thing to draw someone's attention to people as a gift of God!). The elder was using the power of example to encourage John. He encourages John with their victory through persecution, their having been washed in the blood of the Lamb, their service of God, their security in the safekeeping of God, their satisfaction in the presence of God, and the presence of Jesus their great shepherd!

One of the tremendous benefits of teamwork is the power of example. I remember serving on committees with men and women who were faithfully following Jesus in very difficult circumstances. I remember watching them sacrifice much as they adopted children from foreign countries. I remember being encouraged by the way they responded to difficulties. As I write this chapter, there is a woman in our church who takes care of her ailing husband. After decades of marriage, many spouses look at the other and say, "Serve me." But not her. She rises early before the sun and stays up late so that she can faithfully serve her husband. I want to be like that. I want to love my wife that way. I'm so glad that God has put me on the same team as her so that I can be encouraged by her example!

The Plurality of Praise

John's vivid description of heaven leaves us no doubt about the centrality of praise. Heaven is an active worship session that is focused on the redeeming work of God through Christ. And rightly so. But what we can easily miss is the plurality of this praise. It is never just one person. There are no solos in heaven.

In Revelation 4 we see four living creatures around the throne. Each described in some detail. Each individually unique. And beautifully together. In Heaven we are better able to proclaim the excellences of God together than we are independent of others. Why would it be any different on earth? We need each other. Teamwork that intentionally aims for the glory of God embraces this. Whether it is the orchestra that comes together to produce music or the Christian school board that comes together to make guiding decision for the school, we need each other. We ought not rob God of glory because we, in our pride, don't want to value those around us.

In Isaiah 6 we see a plurality of seraphim worshipping. And Isaiah points out, "And one called to another and said: 'Holy, Holy, Holy is the LORD of hosts; the whole earth is full of his glory!'" Why would they call out "one to another?" Because there are certain realities, even truths about God, which we are better able to receive from others than we are on our own. It is a gift to sing with the local church. It is a gift to hear others pray. It is a gift to worship in community. It is a gift to experience this plurality of praise.

This is one of the reasons that if you are able to walk into a church gathering one Sunday morning and simply go through the entire church gathering without seeing the face of another worshipper in the room, it's an unhealthy experience. Christian, in Heaven you will forever enjoy God in the company of others. Begin that today. So how can the team you currently serve on point you to this reality? How can you begin to experience the grace of God in their company?

The Certainty of the Outcome

Undoubtedly John wanted the readers of his Revelation to be encouraged about the certainty of the outcome. The lamb would — not *might* — receive the reward of his suffering. The King would — not *possibly* — have his rightful place on the throne and no enemy would stop him. The outcome is secure and certain. John wrote that we might know this. As many hard to interpret messages as Revelation might include, this one is clear. As a youth pastor I would tell students that they could sum up the wonderful message of Revelation in two simple, yet deeply beautiful words: *Jesus wins*.

Does that certainty saturate your teamwork? When we are overwhelmed by this certainty, we are not tossed about by the waves of uncommitted team-members or completely derailed when the team fails to achieve the results we expected. Think about the last time your team was judged on a project or result that did not turn out the way you hoped. Were you and the other team members crushed? While a level of remorse and resolve to improve in future endeavors is quite appropriate, despondency is not. Or think about a time that your team knocked the project out of the proverbial ballpark. Rejoicing is appropriate. But pride is not. The certainty of Jesus' victory puts both our failures and successes in the proper perspective. The gospel, and the sure outcome of the gospel, frees us to teamwork.

It's true. Jesus does win. Heaven is real. The Bible tells me so. So let us work together to fill up heaven with worshippers from every nation, tribe, people, and language. Work in such a way that those who served on a team with you will offer rich and deep praise. Whatever role you play on the team and whatever arena your team serves in, be a team player for the glory of God. I asked our congregation one Sunday morning after singing the great hymn "Holy, Holy, Holy," if at the end of that year those words would mean more to the people around them because of their interaction? Let it be so. That is the point of teamwork: to glorify God and enjoy him forever.

Team Discussion Questions

1. God has delighted to use teams in his mission. How does this truth lead you to more deeply cherish teamwork and possibly repent of the moments in which you treated teamwork with a spirit of complacency or even neglect?

2. Who are some Christians whose example is a bright encouragement to you?

3. Jeff wrote, "there are no solos in heaven." How does the plurality of praise that occurs in heaven impact your view of, and participation in, teamwork?

ELEVEN

If I Have Not Love . . .

"If I have prophetic powers, and understand all mysteries and all knowledge, and if I have all faith, so as to remove mountains, but have not love, I am nothing" (1 Corinthians 13:2).

Teamwork matters to God. It is a chief tool that he uses in conforming us into the image of his Son. God's aim in putting you on a team with others is that you would look more like Jesus for your time spent with them, and that they might look more like Jesus for their time spent with you. You didn't just get assigned to that project or placed in that new work building. God put you there. God placed you on that team. And his purpose for you there is love.

Healthy teamwork hangs on love. If we have the greatest team strategy, the best looking team members (you're on it after all!), the most compelling mission statement, the dream team of dream teams, but have not love . . . we have nothing.

Teams could reword Paul's thirteenth chapter in First Corinthians,

"If I speak in the tongues of excellent leaders and captivating speakers,

> but have not love,

I am a grinding gear or an annoying light fixture hum."

"And if I have perfect team strategy and understand all personality profiles and all thought processes, and if I have all confidence and optimism,

> but have not love,

I am nothing."

"If I am the best team leader, first to arrive and last to leave, and if I sacrifice more than everyone else on the team combined,

> but have not love,

I gain nothing."

Love is the outworking of Christ in us as we serve on teams. As we sit down after a long week to serve for a few hours on the local school board. As we meet with our co-workers at the office to rehash the latest failed project. As we bite our tongues while we're publicly berated by the office bully. Love that is patient and kind.

Love is the humility that celebrates when another team member achieves the long-sought after success that they've been working towards. Love honors others and points out the value in their ideas and contributions rather than feeling threatened. Love does not need to celebrate itself because it is so happy to celebrate others.

Love never ends. So, by all means let us employ the most recent wisdom and business acumen as we serve on teams. Let's take the latest personality profile and finally know which Star Wars character we are most like. Let us understand how our personalities mesh and clash with others and let us find our strengths. But let us be marked primarily by love. All of these tests will fade away and will be replaced by the next wave of knowledge . . . but love never ends.

As you've processed a biblical vision of teamwork throughout this book, I hope that you have been pointed repeatedly to Jesus Christ who so loved us that he gave his life for us. I hope that you have found yourself not just thinking about what you need to do but marveling at what God has done in Christ for you. I hope that you have been a recipient of love through this book.

And having received the love of God in Christ, go. Be a team member who bears the image of a triune God who has operated in teamwork from eternity past. Go. Remember the example of Moses *and* . . . and all that God accomplished through his servants such as David, Nehemiah, and Deborah. Walk wisely as you think about the outworking of godly teamwork in your life and as you hear the prophetic call to teamwork. Go, knowing that Jesus himself called broken team members and gladly walked with them, bearing their burdens in love. See the mighty acts of the Holy Spirit sweeping through the early church and hear Pauls' exemplary celebration of team. Allow the beauty of heaven to captivate you and call you to teamwork.

And above all these, as you serve on teams, as you continue to grow in grace and truth, be a person who is overwhelmingly, radically, and wildly driven by *love*.

Jeff Mingee is the lead pastor of Catalyst Church in Newport News, Virginia. Jeff has seen the benefits and blessings of teamwork first hand having served on the Pastoral Team of Bethel Baptist in Yorktown and now leading the team at Catalyst Church. He trains and serves church planters in the Southern Baptist Conservatives of Virginia and has served on the coaching staff of athletic teams in the past. Jeff has a M.Div. from Southeastern Baptist Theological Seminary and a B.A. from Christopher Newport University. Jeff lives in Newport News with his wife, Lauren, and their two sons, Aiden and Carter.

Connect with Jeff:

I really hope this book has been a help to you. I've learned each one of these principles—not in a solitary study, but in teams. I'm a better person and a better follower of Jesus because of the influence of so many people that God has used. If you'd ever like to connect to talk about the principles here, give me a call: 757-812-8951 or write: jwmingee@gmail.com.

Visit
www.ichthuspublications.com
for other gospel-centered books or to publish with us.

Made in the USA
Coppell, TX
06 December 2020